Have
You
Hugged
Your
Teenager
Today?

Have You Hugged Your Teenager Today?

A Six-Point Strategy for Maximizing Love and Minimizing Guilt

Patricia H. Rushford

SPIRE

Published by Fleming H. Revell
a division of Baker Book House Company
P.O Box 6287, Grand Rapids, MI 49516-6287

Spire edition published 1996

Third printing, March 1997

Printed in the United States of America

ISBN 0-8007-8636-X

For current information about all releases from
Baker Book House, visit our web site:

http://www.bakerbooks.com/

TO
Daniel and Caryl

Acknowledgment

A special thanks to my editor, Fritz Ridenour, who patiently helped me turn words into a book.

To Ron, who didn't marry an author, but who ended up with one anyway, and who never asks me to choose between my typewriter and him.

To Ruby MacDonald and Lauraine Snelling, my critique partners, who pushed, encouraged, criticized, and loved me.

To Dave and Caryl for being themselves.

To all the parents of teenagers, who were honest with me and allowed me to use their hurts and hilarities in my book.

Contents

PART I

IT IS POSSIBLE TO PARENT WITHOUT GUILT   13

1 Confessions of a Guilty Parent   15
2 Why Do I Take These Guilt Trips?   23
3 Where Do Those Guilt Trips Come From?   29

PART II

SIX KEY STRATEGIES
FOR COPING WITH GUILT   41

4 Turn on the Power of Positives   43
5 Loosen Up and Laugh   51
6 Turn Your Weakness Into Strength   58
7 Be Real—Not Ideal   69
8 Learn to Be a Good Loser   77
9 Love Your Teenager as Yourself   89

PART III

HUGGING YOUR TEENAGER
THROUGH IT ALL   103

10 Gradual Deparenting *Versus* All-Out Independence 105
11 The Disappearing Teen   117
12 The Food Game   127
13 The Driving Force   137
14 Breaking Away   147

Epilogue: Feathering the Empty Nest   157

Suggested Reading List   160

When parents overflow
    their home with love,
Guilt loses
    its room and board.

PART I

IT IS POSSIBLE TO PARENT WITHOUT GUILT

Most parents of teenagers suffer from guilt. I was no different. In fact, guilt still stifles me on occasion. But, over the years, I've learned some truths about such guilt that I'd like to share with you. These first three chapters will deal with how "The Guilty Parent Blues" began; the discovery of the real enemies and originators of guilt trips; and, finally, some ways to keep from taking them.

Falling into guilt can be as hopeless as tumbling into a large vat of unsweetened chocolate—thick, dark, and bitter. Even if someone rescues you, it takes a long time to wash it all off and repair the emotional damages.

1

Confessions of a Guilty Parent

D-Day—July 16—Day One after our son David's thirteenth birthday.

"Come on, honey. Get your bags packed. We're going to the beach this weekend."

"Not me. I have other plans. It's no fun with you guys anyway. I'll stay at Nana's."

"I . . . ah . . . I don't think so, Dave," I stammered, bewildered by his response.

"I mean it, Mom. I can't stand riding in the car with Caryl, you and Dad. No way! I'm not going."

"But honey, we always have fun at the beach."

"I don't! I'll call Nana."

Stunned by the fresh mouth of my newly commissioned teenager, I pursued him into the kitchen, where he proceeded to dial his grandmother's number.

"Wait a minute," I finally responded. "Don't you think we'd better talk to your dad about this?"

"What for? It's settled. I won't go."

"Don't be too sure. If Dad says you go—you go."

"I can make my own decisions now, Mom. I don't need anybody telling me what to do."

"GOD, DO YOU CARRY A WARRANTY?"

Thus began the first of many confrontations which led me to search laboriously for answers to questions such as:

- What's happening to my children?
- Was it something I said?
- Will life ever be normal again?
- Will I survive?

I thought I knew all about adolescence, but I never dreamed I'd be begging God for a reprieve; yet, here I am, four years and at least a thousand headaches later, still asking my children's Manufacturer for help. I talk to God a lot these days (myself, too, for that matter). In fact, I talk so much, I wonder if He's still listening.

"Hey, God," I'd say, "do You carry a warranty? My kids seem to be malfunctioning."

Actually, sometimes I'm tempted to think the Lord just sits up there and chuckles at me. Experienced parents can be like that, as my mother-in-law proves. When I told her about our troubles with *her* grandson, she laughed and confessed, "I always told Ron he'd have a son just like himself when he grew up—and he did. Now it's my turn to sit back and watch *him* struggle."

Ha! Very funny. Even if Ron deserves to have a kid who misbehaves, do I?

Don't get me wrong. Parenting our children hasn't always been a hardship. In fact, we started out *great.* First, God blessed Ron and me with a warm, wiggly, blue-eyed David; followed two years later by his soft, angel sister, Caryl. Aside from a touch of parental insecurity, sibling rivalry, hyperactivity, and a few minor crises, life bounced along fairly well.

When Dave turned twelve, he started acting a little weird, but it didn't seem too serious. We tried to dismiss it by saying maybe he had a few wires crossed. Unfortunately, things got worse. Eventually, he started getting completely out of line at times. We have struggled diligently to keep him running smoothly. Caryl has been a bit easier. She has only short-circuited a couple of times; but when she's blown, the shock and confusion hits like a total blackout of New York City.

For a while I thought we could handle the problems ourselves. But as they progressed, I found myself calling on God more and more often for help. It's obvious that some of the intricate parts making up these kids is classified information. Since God is the one with the blueprints, I'll have to leave the repair work to Him. While we wait for God to make His repairs, we have to live with our teenagers and their changes.

My mother said, "The problems you and Ron are having with Dave and Caryl are normal. Most teenagers are afflicted."

"If that's true," I moaned, "why didn't you warn us? We could have avoided the problem by adopting twenty-year-olds. Besides, I didn't give you any trouble as a teenager, did I?"

Mother just smiled.

WHY HAS GUILT ALWAYS HOUNDED ME?

Mother's smile indicated I might have been a slightly less than perfect teenager, but it seemed to me that she didn't have half the battles with me as I've had with David and Caryl. All this definitely leads me to believe I must have a few flaws in my parenting theories.

Oh, I tried reading all the experts—some secular, some Christian. I'll always be grateful to Dr. James Dobson and the Reverend Charles Swindoll for pointing me back to the basic book for child rearing—the Bible. Still, I must confess, even with all the reading, I wound up feeling more and more confused and guilty. I was really bothered about all those errors I made when I didn't know any better.

For example, Dr. Dobson, who became my new hero with books like *The Strong-Willed Child* and *Hide or Seek,* made me hang my head in shame over the "Barbie Doll" syndrome. He said in *Hide or Seek,* "There could be no better method for teaching the worship of beauty and materialism than is done with luscious Barbie. . . ."

I appreciated his advice, but where was he ten years ago? My little girl grew up with curvaceous Barbie. No wonder she complains about her straight-line form. "I feel like a fifteen-year-old trapped inside the body of a ten-year-old. And these pimples.... *Ugh!* Mom! What went wrong?"

That's what I'd like to know. What went wrong? As I continued to reflect on my children's earlier years, more guilt-producing errors surfaced. For instance, if I told a modern pediatrician that I nursed Dave for only three months before switching him to cow's milk, he'd probably accuse me of contributing to the delinquency of a minor. But, how was I to know cow's milk didn't digest well in baby's tiny tummy?

Not only that, I pushed the potty training before he turned two. Grandma told me to get him trained before the next baby came, or I'd have two in diapers. Horrors! Maybe Dave wouldn't be so temperamental if I'd been more patient.

Oh, and poor Caryl was never nursed and had to start life with Playtex nursers, the "next best thing" to Mommy.

But those are all minor points. I guess the major cause for a lot of my guilt feelings concerning our teenagers has been my temper. Boy, can I get angry. According to Freud, I may have damaged the kids' psyches beyond repair—permanently bruised them. I thank God the temper flare-ups are more easily controlled now (most of the time), but I still feel like an ogress.

"YUK, DO WE HAVE TO EAT EGGS?"

I had one explosion that was so violent, it gave me enough guilt to last for a decade. The eruption occurred when Dave was eleven years old, and Caryl was nine.

I crawled out of bed and groped my way to the kitchen at 6:30 that morning to fix the children some breakfast. I'd worked till midnight the night before. Sure, I suffered from exhaustion, but I wanted to give my darlings a special treat. Besides, if I didn't cook breakfast, guilt would sock me in like a dense fog.

I cooked eggs, toast, bacon, and hashbrowns—the works. Caryl made her entrance with a "Yuk, do we have to eat eggs?"

David chimed in with, "I wanted my eggs whole, not scrambled."

I don't know how you are in the morning, but before tea, my brain functions at a slightly less than rational level. With unleashed hostility, I yanked a wooden spoon out of the drawer and shook it at them.

"You eat what's put before you. I could still be sleeping; but instead, I'm out here slaving over a hot stove, so *you* can go to school with a hot breakfast instead of cold cereal." Cr-a-ck-ck! The spoon hit the table. Its top half sailed halfway across the kitchen.

I shoved their plates at them and pitched a fork into the sink. *Cr-a-a-sh!* I turned, just in time to watch my only large, glass bowl disintegrate into hundreds of free-falling fragments.

A muffled scream forced its way through my tightly set jaw. I closed my eyes and smoldered. *Control yourself,* my brain commanded. My knuckles whitened as I clung to the counter. *Now, take a deep breath,* continued Brain. *Don't let this thing beat you.* Obediently, I breathed deep, opened my eyes, and tried again.

I pushed a milk carton into the fridge and slammed the door. A threatening thud from inside the big, white box told me I still had troubles. I pulled open the door to a milk flood. Milk gushed, endlessly, from the tipped half-gallon container, drenching my bare feet and kitchen carpet.

Tears poured down my hot, red face. I savagely grabbed for towels and with hostile vengeance beat on the milk-saturated carpet. Cleanup and tears finally subdued my anger. I looked up at two innocent grade-schoolers, who stared, possum-eyed in wonder that a mother could fall to such a devastating display of violence.

Guilt devoured me. What had I done? I couldn't let them go to school until I apologized, convinced them I wasn't crazy, and assured them with "I love yous." They didn't need to apologize. I knew they were sorry they'd even opened their mouths.

Never, in all my life, had I exploded with such fury. Talk about blowing your top. It took me days to recuperate.

"Oh, Lord," I cried. "You've got to help me control this temper. Please don't let me get angry like that again."

Fortunately, the Lord has helped me curb my temper, but it's in constant need of repair. Every so often, I have a minor blowout, and it's back to God's repair shop for an overhaul. Maybe someday I'll be able to remain calm in any situation. (I'm sure it won't be until my teenagers are grown and gone.)

A CHILD LEARNS WHAT HE LIVES (OUCH!)

Now maybe you understand why I still feel guilty. I'm haunted by questions such as:

- Did my anger produce anger in my teenagers?
- Am I to blame?
- And what about resentment; am I responsible for that too?
- Ron and I have tried to be good parents. Why do I feel like a failure?

One reason for my inferiority as a parent stems from a cute little poster I've seen hanging around—the one entitled *A Child Learns What He Lives.*

> If a child lives with criticism,
>   He learns to condemn.
> If a child lives with hostility,
>   He learns to fight.
> If a child lives with shame,
>   He learns to feel guilty.
> If a child lives with tolerance,
>   He learns to be patient.

> If a child lives with encouragement,
>> He learns confidence.
> If a child lives with praise,
>> He learns to appreciate.
> If a child lives with fairness,
>> He learns justice.
> If a child lives with security,
>> He learns to have faith.
> If a child lives with approval,
>> He learns to like himself.
> If a child lives with acceptance and friendship,
>> He learns to find love in the world.
>
> DOROTHY LAW NOLTE

I couldn't hang that poster in my house because it made me feel too guilty. Every time one of my children shows up with a negative trait, I think it must be my fault.

Is Dave critical today because I told him, "I don't care if it is a sports banquet; you can't wear your swim trunks and a tank-top"? Is Caryl impatient because I couldn't tolerate a three-day shopping spree for one pair of shoes?

I could go on and on about my failures at motherhood, but guilt would undoubtedly multiply itself. If only I could say, "Guilt, be gone!" and it would vanish, never to intrude my parental soul again. Unfortunately, guilt roots itself too deeply to be chased away in a day.

GOD FORGIVES, BUT ...

In my desire to uproot guilt, I did try simply to ask God for forgiveness. According to the Bible, "If we confess our sins, he is faithful and just, and will forgive our sins and cleanse us from all unrighteousness" (1 John 1:9).

Knowing this, I prayed:

Lord, You tell me if I confess my sins, You will forgive me. Well, I'm asking forgiveness for all the mistakes I made as a parent. Anger, impatience, selfishness (getting wrapped up in my own activities instead of theirs), spankings that shouldn't have been, things I thought about (like punching my boy in the mouth, but didn't, only because he's stronger than I am), and anything else I might have done to damage my children. *There.* I'm all confessed.

"Confession equals forgiveness." You said it Yourself, Lord.

Allelulia! I'm forgiven! The slate is wiped clean. I've been freed of guilt and can leave it behind.

I'm not guilty.

> *I'm not guilty!*
> > I'M NOT GUILTY!

. . . *Ahem* . . . Lord? The Bible assures me I'm forgiven. Guilt is no longer a problem between us—right? Then why do I still *feel* guilty?

As I pondered this guilt dilemma I seemed to be in, I began to wonder: Am I the only one who feels that way? How many guilty parents are there in the world? I'd heard rumors, but knew of only a few. I guess guilt is one of those hush-hush topics. After all, confession of guilt feelings might implicate us as responsible for pushing our children into the depths of rebellion.

In my heart, I felt a strong urge to talk about my teenage trouble with a friend or two with whom I could sing my "Guilty Parent Blues," but not until I found a few more so-called guilty parents. Fortunately, I didn't have to look far. In fact, I hit a "motherload."

2

Why Do I Take These Guilt Trips?

Eagerly, I began my search for parents, who, like me, suffered from "The Guilty Parent Blues." Success came quickly.

Since I work as a registered nurse in a Pediatric Emergency Clinic, I found plenty of parents among my co-workers to question. My sources proved not only valid but plentiful. I uncovered enough guilt to open a Guilt Shop and keep us miserably in business for two thousand years.

Several other nurses and physicians, also moms and dads, talked freely with me during a lunch break.

"Does anybody else feel guilty about their kids, or am I in this alone?" I began.

CONFESSIONS AT THE CLINIC

"You're not alone," confessed Jean, also a registered nurse. "Everytime my teenagers are unhappy, I feel like a failure. If I say *no* to any of their demands, I'm diagnosed as overbearing, overprotective, cold-blooded and unfeeling. Before the ordeal is over, I've fallen head over heels in guilt."

"Yes," chuckled Dr. Allen, head of the Pediatric Clinic. "I told my daughter she couldn't buy any new clothes for at least two months. I thought she was going to die on the spot. She went into withdrawals."

"Did you feel guilty?"

"No, but my wife did. I can't prove it, but I think she bought her a pair of socks to give her a fix."

"Very funny. Are you saying men don't feel guilty? Is this ailment for women only?"

"I think women generally feel more guilt than men—at least where children are concerned. Maybe we just don't have enough time to think about it. The one thing I do feel guilty about though, is the lack of time I spend with my kids."

"My husband has the same problem," I admitted. "He's always saying he should take Dave fishing or play more games with him."

"You're kidding," chided Jean. "Isn't he the one who sits for hours watching them do their gymnastics. You guys go more places together than any family I know. I think he's feeling guilty over nothing."

"Hmmm . . . manufactured guilt. He'll be glad to hear that. I suppose if we cross the 'lack of time crime' off his list, he'll find another shameful guilt trip to take its place. Anybody else care to confess the guilties?"

"Spankings," shared Karen, a nurses' aide. "I feel guilty every time I spank my kids. Especially when I get mad and yell at them. Their big, tear-filled eyes look up at me in pure innocence. I feel awful—and they know it."

Nods of agreement spread around the room.

"Time and lack of patience," Chris, our receptionist added. "I should pay more attention to my kids. Sometimes I feel like I'm cheating them. I get so busy with housework and laundry—ugh! I do as many as ten loads a day. They can't understand why Mommy can't read to them every time they ask. When I do sit down with them, my patience fades fast. What do you do when your three-year-old wants to read, and his eighteen-month-old brother keeps chewing on the books?"

"How about you Dr. Hanson," I asked. "Are you guilt-ridden like the rest of us?"

"And how! Got about ten years? I'll try to condense it. I was too young and immature when I got married. Consequently, I don't feel I gave Jerry the care he should have had," Dr. Hanson, the Pediatric Resident, confessed of her relationship with her ten-year-old son. "To make matters worse, when he was sixteen months old, his father and I divorced. Then I was too busy feeling sorry for myself to mother him adequately.

"My problem isn't so much the guilt over my shortcomings then," she continued, "because now, I'm okay, but, my kid won't let me forget it. He's not about to give up the one tool he knows is effective. I get the feeling he plans out his strategies in advance. If I say *no,* he subtly reminds me, 'If we had a dad, things would be different.' I feel guilty and can't refuse him. Kids are no dummies; they know where you hurt."

Sarah, also a nurse, agreed with Dr. Hanson and shared similar feelings of guilt and helplessness with her son, seven-year-old Ryan. "At times Ryan confronts me with questions like, 'Why did you leave my daddy? Doesn't he need us to take care of him?'

"I feel like I should have tried harder to keep my marriage together. It hurts to be reminded. I don't think he's using guilt against me though—do you?"

"If he's not, I'll bet he's accumulating the ammunition," Dr. Hanson answered. "It won't be long."

"I wouldn't be surprised," I reflected. "Dave accuses us ruthlessly, 'If you and Dad hadn't yelled at me and punished me for all those dumb little things I did, I wouldn't get in trouble now.' "

"That's a cop-out!" Dr. Allen exclaimed. "I wouldn't let him get away with that. Make him accept responsibility for his own actions."

"We try," I defended, "but I'm sure he knows, deep down, we feel directly responsible for his behavior."

Although we had to break up our meeting and return to work, our conversations continued throughout the day. I was excited to find so many parents, who were willing to share their guilts and other problems they'd encountered in rearing their children.

Sharing with other parents made me feel much better about the whole guilt complex. And, as a bonus, I realized Ron and I weren't doing such a bad job of bringing up our offspring. Knowing I wasn't alone eased much of the tension I'd been under. Through our discussion, I recognized one important detail about our children, which I had previously overlooked.

MASTERS OF THE GUILT TRIP

Our children would make great travel agents. They are masters at sending us on wild guilt trips. The strategy and perseverance needed to gather information on "What makes Mom and Dad feel most guilty, and how can I use it to get my way?" requires intelligence and skill. Anyone with that much brain power is bound to make it in this world—regardless of whether or not they were nursed.

Why, I wondered, *do kids so often choose to pretend they are a mirror image of only the negative aspects of our personalities?*

The corners of my mouth turned up to a wry smile, as I pictured one of my kids saying, "Yes, I won first place in the athletic competition. However, I feel, in all fairness, I must give all the credit of my success to my kind and considerate parents. Their patience and consistency got me to practice every day. They gave up their valuable time and instilled in me those positive attitudes, without which I'd never have made it."

It's as though most of our children's good qualities mysteriously appeared or were wholly manufactured by their own efforts. According to *them,* parents rarely have anything to do with their good characteristics. But, of course, if they foul things up, young people are the first to admit parents are to blame—at least until they become parents.

After my "share your guilt" session with other parents at the clinic, I ran across a quote from a young college graduate, featured in a reader's survey in *McCalls* magazine (May 1978), which said, "If a kid goes wrong, in most cases it is not the fault of the clergy, the schools or the child's peers. It is the parent's fault."

I'm not sure how *you* react to this bit of collegiate wisdom, but *I* couldn't buy it—at least not all of it.

The way I see it, the blame needs to be shared equally by television, peer pressure, the moral decline of our society, secular humanism, role changes, specialization, urbanization, so-called uninhibited movies, the high divorce rate—and the beat goes on. I, for one, was not about to buy a one-way ticket on any Guilt Trip Express because of games the younger generation was trying to play with my head.

WHY ALL THE GUILT FEELINGS?

At the same time, however, I still had loads of guilt feelings, and while some of them were real, I had a strong hunch a lot of them were false. False or not, all the guilt seemed very real to me.

So how, I wondered, *do I, and guilt-ridden parents like me,* get rid of all this unwanted, fabricated guilt? Before I could deal with that question, I needed to gather a little more information on guilt itself. First, I checked with God.

"Lord," I asked earnestly, "how can I tell the difference between real and false guilt?"

Since God didn't send His answers booming down over the airwaves, I suspected He felt the problem had been covered sufficiently in the Bible and other accountable books, so I started digging.

I found a great definition in a book called *Guilt and Grace* by Paul Tournier (Harper & Row): ". . . 'false guilt' is that which comes as a result of the judgement and suggestion of men. 'True guilt' is that which results from divine judgement."

Another book *Freedom from Guilt* (Vision House) made the separation even clearer. The authors, Bruce Narramore and Bill Counts, term false guilt as "psychological guilt" and true guilt as "constructive sorrow" or conviction.

"Psychological guilt produces self-inflicted misery," Counts and Narramore said.

That described a lot of *my* guilt all right. It stemmed from feelings of worthlessness, failure, self-rejection and low self-esteem. Whenever I thought I failed in the job expected of me as a parent, I suffered from false guilt. When I persecuted myself and cried, "It's all my fault," I wallowed in it.

The next step, obviously, was to learn how to tell real guilt from false (psychological) guilt. I got more help from Counts and Narramore, who said: "God never makes a Christian feel psychological guilt. . . .

"Constructive sorrow produces a positive change of behavior. . . . Conviction simply means that God is clearly showing us our sins and admonishing us to change."

In other words, if we really do something wrong, God lets us know. Not by guilt or fear of punishment, but by conviction and a call to turn from sin. We then go on to ask forgiveness and make the necessary changes in our lives. Nowhere in the Bible does God tell us to punish ourselves over and over again with guilt and remorse for our past sins. Paul does talk about having sorrow for sin—the good kind of sorrow God wants us to have, "For God sometimes uses sorrow in our lives to help us turn away from sin . . ." (2 Corinthians 7:10 TLB).

True guilt then is when the Holy Spirit uses our conscience to tell us we've sinned. The godly sorrow makes us want to change.

False guilt is when we feel burdened and worthless—without scriptural basis. False guilt tears down our self-worth and causes our conscience to nurture our guilts and blow them out of proportion.

As I studied Tournier, Counts, Narramore, and Paul, I began to get the picture, but I had one more problem to work out. Just where did all this guilt come from? But, before we get to that, let's take definite steps to eliminate those real guilts right now.

STEPS TOWARD GUILT-FREE PARENTING

1. Make a list of the guilts that plague you. Label them *Godly Sorrow, False Guilt,* and *Unknown.*

2. Take a look at the first column—*Godly Sorrows*. These again are actions or sins you know to be wrong, according to Scripture. Now, confess these sins, apologize to the one you sinned against. Repent and receive God's divine forgiveness. You're forgiven— now forgive yourself.

3. If a few of the guilts you had labeled *Godly Sorrows* are still haunting you, move them over to the *False Guilt* list. (If they are still haunting you, they are probably not real *Godly Sorrows*.)

4. Now, tear off the list of *Godly Sorrows* and burn them. God has blotted them from His mind—you can too.

5. Bundle up all those other pesky, burdensome guilts, *False* and *Unknown* and carry them over to chapter 3. There you'll be exposed to some of the sources of false guilt and find out what you can do to combat them.

3

Where Do Those Guilt Trips Come From?

As I continued my probe of guilt, both false and real, I encountered Ruth, a dear friend, who is the mother of four grown children. Ruth claimed unbearable guilt over anger she felt toward her oldest daughter, Karen, while she was a teenager. Karen is now thirty, happily married with a two-year-old son, and probably developing a guilt complex of her own. Ruth would cry at the mention of her daughter's name. She wrote letters of apology to Karen regularly. Conversations between the two were awkward and heavy with Ruth's remorse. Karen accepted her mom's apology years ago and tried repeatedly to reassure her mom that she didn't need to feel guilty.

Even I, a novice guilt reducer, and a veteran hoarder of heavy guilts, could expose Ruth's guilt trip as a counterfeit.

"You don't need to feel guilty," I declared.

"But I can't help it," cried Ruth. "I feel responsible."

"Ruth," I consoled, "let's take a good look at this guilt trip you're on. Maybe this stuff I've been reading can help. First of all, were you angry all the time, or did you show her you loved her?"

"Oh, I would just get angry once in a while. She used to make me so mad. Of course when it all blew over, I always made up with her and hugged her—when she'd let me."

"Ruth, where did you get the idea that getting angry was so wrong. I mean ... Jesus got angry in the temple didn't He?"

"Yes ... I guess He did."

"As I see it, maybe anger isn't the greatest way to handle a child who refuses to listen to you or who disrespectfully talks back to you; but doggone, we're only human. Sometimes tempers flare. The Bible allows that in us. 'Be angry but do not sin; do not let the sun go down on your anger, and give no opportunity to the devil' (Ephesians 4:26)."

"You're right," smiled Ruth through glistening tears. "Maybe I've been punishing myself, and all this time I really believed God was punishing me. I thought I was *supposed* to feel guilty."

"You asked God's forgiveness for those angry scenes years ago, right?" Ruth nodded. "And you asked your daughter's forgiveness?" Again she nodded in affirmation. "Then I think it's time to forgive yourself. It seems to me all this guilt you've got built up inside is hurting the good relationship you could have with Karen. After all, who wants to be around someone who is continually saying, 'I'm sorry.' I guess if you were my mom, I'd feel guilty because you felt guilty. And, in my opinion, that's not healthy."

"You know," admitted Ruth, "I think you're right."

Ruth had refused forgiveness for her anger and allowed guilt feelings to drive her into neurotic despair. She had also unknowingly built up a wall between herself and her daughter.

It was easy to help Ruth with *her* problem. *Maybe,* I mused, *I should go into psychiatry.* On second thought, I knew better. If I didn't start handling my own false guilts with a little more skill, I'd be in psychiatry all right—on a couch.

As I thought about Ruth's problem—and my own—I wrestled again with the question, "Where does false guilt come from?" I continued my research with renewed fervor. Before long, I discovered at least four major sources of the false guilt that hovers over our parental heads like a hungry vulture.

IT ALL STARTED WITH OUR OWN PARENTS

As I remembered Ruth's battle with guilt and how she unknowingly passed her guilts along to her daughter, I realized that guilt often originates as a family affair.

Feelings are born in childhood, as we learn which of our behaviors are acceptable and which are not. The amount of guilt and reasons we feel guilty stem out of responses of our parents and other family members toward our behavior. There are reward-producing and punishment-producing behaviors.

Most of us, at one time or another, were punished out of parental anger and frustration. "Shame on you," has been a favorite scold among parents for years. Some parents even resort to withholding love as a means of punishment when the child fails to act properly.

These parental actions can produce fear, low self-esteem, and feelings of rejection in the child. Remember back to chapter 2? These are the basis for our psychological guilt.

It would seem that parents are largely responsible for the production of guilt feelings within us. But, if we blame *our* parents, and they blame *their* parents, it would only take us back to Adam and Eve, and that won't solve our guilt problem either.

Our parents were only doing what they thought was right by

societal standards of their day; just as we strive to do what is right with the knowledge we have today.

As a child, I remember the often-spoken words, "Jesus loves you when you're good." I surmised in my clever little head that if Jesus loves good little girls, He didn't like me sometimes. Talk about fear and rejection! I was afraid God would ban me from heaven if I looked sideways at my brother. So I tried and tried to live up to Jesus' standards. It took years before I finally discovered God loves me even when I'm rotten.

Just as my parents instilled a few guilties in me, I've done my share in adding to my children's repertoire of guilt stories. I'm sure my angry remarks like: "Can't I count on you for anything?"; or "After all I've done for you ..."; or "Go to your room and stay there." Oh, and then there's the old "How *could* you?"; and "Must you *always* ... ?" Ouch! It hurts to be reminded I actually said things like that. I never wanted to hurt my children, and my parents never wanted to hurt me; but here we all are, partners in Guilt Unlimited, Inc.

AND THEN THE EXPERTS CHIMED IN

While we, our parents, our parents' parents (and so on), are accountable for some of the initial guilt, a portion of parental guilt is born out of our conscience, as we read the latest psychological trends on child rearing. As I mentioned before, every book or article I read pointed out my mistakes.

For years, psychiatrists have made a fortune selling books that tell us the right way to raise our children, so they would grow up wonderfully obedient, respectful, and emotionally healthy. If we follow their instructions precisely, we should come out with perfectly well-behaved children. Of course, these same "experts" remain available to treat our neuroses or psychoses (alias guilt complex) when we fail.

Don't misunderstand me. I'm not saying you shouldn't read "how-to-parent" books. I'm simply saying, if you decide to read these books, take into account "human error," on the part of yourself, your spouse, your children, and the author.

Psychiatrists aren't the only guilt producers. Parents have been taught for generations by well-meaning doctors, ministers, social workers, and others, that when a child misbehaves or goes wrong, the parent is ultimately at fault.

Lest you think I'm paranoid, let me share with you a few quotes and ideas from people who strongly believe in parental guilt.

Just recently the *Seattle Times* editorial page carried a headline SCHOOL DISCIPLINE: PARENTS ARE CRUX OF THE PROBLEM. The article was written by a senior-high-school counselor, who indicated parents should be held entirely responsible for the conduct of their children in schools. My question is "Does this mean teachers are to take *no* responsibility for discipline in the school?" Horsefeathers!

> Delinquent parents beget delinquent children; good parents rear good children. Of course, there are exceptions but these are rare and society could easily cope with them. By overcoming and correcting adult delinquency we can greatly reduce the delinquency of children.

Feel guilty? Or perhaps like me, you felt a twinge of anger. That statement was made by J. Edgar Hoover, former head of the FBI, in a publication from the FBI "Uniform Crime Report," quoted by David Wilkerson in *Parents on Trial* (Spire).

True, parents must accept some responsibility for the behavior of their children, but to let the so-called experts ride herd on us with guilt, why—it's inhuman. As long as we let these experts nail us with this bum rap, we'll be labeled GUILTY AS CHARGED. I think it's time we parents came to our own defense

OUR PEERS DO THEIR FAIR SHARE

It all began with our own parents, then the experts chimed in, and then our peers do their fair share. Yes, our *peers*.

Friends and co-parents often shower us with guilt, and much of the time they don't even realize it.

As I talked with friends about guilt and teenage troubles, I most often found empathy. However, I did run across a few exceptions. After my successful encounter at work, I bravely ventured out to try my sharing technique on a few peers in a Sunday school class.

We were each asked to share with the class a specific problem which frequently distressed us. What an opportunity!

After the leader, Ellen, and her sidekick, Mary, spoke up, I plunged in. I should have known better, but I neglected to read the signals: DANGER! NO DIVING! COMMUNICATION LEVEL TOO SHALLOW!

Ellen had confided, "My problem is, I never find time to pamper myself. I'm forever doing things for my children."

Mary openly admitted, "I can't lose weight. This extra five pounds simply refuses to budge. I suppose it comes from preparing all that extra food for my teenage son."

I had already started feeling guilty. I have time for myself— maybe I'm not spending enough time on the children? And preparing extra food? If the kids don't eat what I make, that's tough ... hmmm ... maybe I should do a little more work in the kitchen. Oh, well, I'll deal with this case of guilt later.

In the meantime, being next in line, I boldly confessed, "I lose my temper with my teenagers too easily." A quick glance around the room told me I'd drifted too far from shore. My honest remarks were met with silent lips and shouting eyes: *Unclean! Unclean! Poor fallen creature.*

After a brief silence, I shifted in my chair and continued speaking, in an attempt to row myself closer to shore. "I practically got into a wrestling match with my son this morning, trying to get him to church." I thought maybe the word *church* would bring me back into their good graces. When their looks remained unchanged, my boldness melted. I finished my short-lived "show and tell" with a humble, "I hate it when anger gets the best of me."

Silence ensued.

Angie, a faithful friend, finally came to my aid. "I lose my temper sometimes too." Then she meekly injected, "I know what you mean."

The initial shock had worn off most of the faces and blank expressions guarded feelings. I couldn't tell if they were stunned or sympathetic—that is, except for Ellen and Mary. Their countenances shifted. Patronizing glances told me they had found a fallen sister and were about to help me back into the fold.

"Do you think it's wise to push your teenagers to the point of anger in yourself or them?" Ellen cooed. "I believe children are more cooperative when allowed to make decisions for themselves. Heaven knows, I never forced my Jenny to do anything she didn't want to. Consequently, we never disagree. And Jenny is an angel."

Good for you, I wanted to shout, but wisely held my words. ... (*Sigh.*) Here it comes—more guilt. I already carry enough guilt around to fill a dozen trunks, and here I am, cornered by two lovely Christian ladies, who unknowingly load me up with more.

"Oh," Mary soothed, "I'm sure we've all been angry with our kids a time or two. Why, I remember once about nine years ago...."

Nine years ago? I tuned out Mary's futile attempt to empathize. How can anyone control their temper for nine years? Maybe there really *is* something wrong with me. My self-worth took a tumble as I picked up her last words. "... of course, that was before I took the class on 'How to Control Your Emotions.' It was easy. Anyone can do it."

Once I escaped the guilt brigade, I decided to retaliate by proving Ellen wrong. I figured without discipline, Ellen's darling Jenny would be a terror. Right? Wrong. After Jenny watching instead of sermon listening for a church hour, I assented to Ellen's claim. Jenny was an angel.

Guilt hemmed me in. My parental self-image plummeted. Convinced of my failure, I moaned, "This temper's turned my teenagers into tyrants."

Just as I slipped under for the second time, Angie appeared from behind and gave my saggy shoulders a firm squeeze. "Hey. Thanks for sharing this morning. Ah, don't let them get you down. So you have a temper—me too. Maybe we can work on it together, like Tempers Anonymous. We're not so bad, you know. Along with our tempers we have a few other intense emotions—like enthusiasm—and laughter—vitality—and lots and lots of love."

"But what about Jenny? Maybe Ellen's right."

"Come on! Jenny would be her compliant self, even if she had Jekyll-Hyde for a father. And, besides, she's only fourteen. Give her a chance. She could still turn."

While some peers are available, whether knowingly or unknowingly, to pick you apart, there are others around, like Angie, to pick you up. Subtle accusations from a peer can cut deeper than words from an expert's pen, or even from our past. When the apparent success of one parent is pitted against the seeming failure of another, guilt usually escalates in the loser. Personally, I think it's time parents banded together to fight guilt, rather than engage in political guilt slinging.

SATAN—SPECIALIST IN FALSE GUILT

On and on weaves the tangled web of guilt. As you see, it all started with our parents; then the experts chimed in; our peers follow through with their fair share—and Satan comes along to finish us off. It's true. I think the final and most deceitful element in guilt production is Satan. Just as God uses our conscience as a tool to bring us to godly, constructive sorrow, Satan utilizes our conscience to produce false guilt.

Satan is an expert in the use of clever guises to entrap us well-meaning parents. Say, for example, you caught your six-year-old son running after and jumping onto a moving milk truck. I don't know how you would react, but I gave Dave a couple of sound swats. Instantly, Satan gasped, "You should never spank your children." (He'd successfully pricked my conscience and come up with an old memory which lingered from a book by one of the experts.)

"But God says in Proverbs 22:15, 'Foolishness is bound up in the heart of a child, but the rod of discipline will drive it far from him' (MLB)," I defended, thinking my Bible knowledge would turn him off.

"Barbaric! If you were a better mother, you wouldn't need to resort to these brutal methods."

"He deserved a spanking. He could have been killed, jumping off that truck. He needed to learn a lesson."

"Still your fault. It wouldn't have happened if you'd been watching him as you should," Satan purred.

Zap! Suddenly I'm caught in his deceptive trap, with no apparent means of escape. How can I fight this invisible force? He's too cunning. I'm often entrapped before I know what's happened.

"So," you may ask, "what did happen?"

I let Satan convince me of my guilt. A guilty conscience is one of the weapons Satan uses to push us into the past and overemphasize our failures. Whenever we see what appears to be ideal parenting, or see ourselves as mistake makers, we hang our heads in shame and guilt consumes us. Satan rejoices in our grief and despair. He knows perfect parenting is a sham, but his job is to keep us dreaming. At the first cry of resentment, anger, or wrongdoing in our children, he moves our hidden guilts into action.

I can almost hear his hollow, malicious laughter bounce off the walls of my brain. "I only plant the idea," he jeers. "As long as you want to go on these guilt trips, I'm more than willing to take you there."

MORE HELP

By now you should have a fairly clear idea of which of your guilts are true and which are false (psychological) guilts. If you are still floating in the *unknown* area, I would suggest you read one or two of the books which cover the guilt matter more thoroughly: *Guilt and Grace* by Paul Tournier; *Freedom from Guilt*, Bruce Narramore and Bill Counts; or *Emotions: Can You Trust Them?* by Dr. James Dobson.

We may never know why we feel guilty or why we feel compelled to blame ourselves or anyone else for the wrong-way turns of our kids. Knowing *why* isn't too important. What is important is to know that God doesn't want us to drown in guilt. Each day, we hold God's gift of a fresh start. We can be forgiven and free of the past. To be guilty or not to be guilty— we make the choice. The trick to guilt-free parenting is to talk our subconscious into dumping the backlog of negative guilt that has accumulated all these years.

As I indicated before, I'm not meaning to take parents off the hook for the responsibility of rearing children. I'm simply pointing out a simple fact: parents can be free from the guilt buildup over past wrongs. And, we are definitely NOT GUILTY in areas of our children's lives over which we have no control.

To blame, criticize, or pass judgment on ourselves or others is futile and even harmful to our physical and spiritual health. As I see it, we have no alternative—guilt must go. True, this deguilting process will take a while.

In the meantime, we need all the help we can get. In the next six chapters we'll discuss six crucial strategies which may help you parent your teenagers with love and without guilt.

As a matter of fact, one of the most important skills I learned is that the best way to decrease guilt in myself is to increase the love I give my kids. Consequently, I make a daily effort to "hug them" in as many ways as I possibly can. How about you? *Have you hugged your teenager today?*

A Plan for Action

Does the whole idea of parenting and guilt seem too gloomy and overwhelming to you? Are you thinking seriously of desertion? Forget it. I've tried to turn in my parent badge a dozen times, but nobody would take it. I simply had to learn an alternative method and fight back.

Conquering this unhealthy emotion—guilt—will take time. You will need goals. Listed below are five goals, which, if consumed in large consistent doses, can direct you into the realm of a *freed parent*.

1. Dwell on the positive qualities in yourself and your children. Take the apostle Paul's advice and ". . . Fix your thoughts on what is true and good and right. Think about things that are pure and lovely and dwell on the fine, good things in others. Think about all you can praise God for and be glad about" (Philippians 4:8, TLB).

2. Stop blaming yourself and others for the negative actions of your children. Stop drowning in past sins and guilt and take affirmative action in the present. Start by escalating your love effort.

3. Refuse to take responsibility for all your child's negative characteristics. Balance the scale by taking responsibility for a few of the good characteristics as well.

4. Do not allow your children the privilege of making you feel guilty over past events or failures.

5. Uplift your parent friends who are in trouble and obey Galatians 6:2, as you seek to "Share each other's troubles and problems . . ." (TLB).

PART II

SIX KEY STRATEGIES FOR COPING WITH GUILT

In the last three chapters you became aware of some major problems with guilt and have seen how to distinguish between godly sorrow and false guilt.

Still, with false guilts bombarding us daily, we wonder, how can we "fight the good fight" as we parent our teenagers. The weight of guilt can inhibit and hinder a parent's effectiveness. At times, I've felt like a mouse caught in an elephant's footprint—with the elephant still standing in it.

With all this guilt weighing me down, I knew I needed to make some changes in my thinking or end up crushed, depressed, and neurotic.

So, change I did. I discovered six simple but practical strategies that helped me cope with guilt, while giving me more freedom to rear my teenagers with love. Once incorporated into a parent's life-style, they become a survival manual. Used consistently, these six strategies can help us muddle through our maze of misdirected energies and misguided emotions.

In the next two chapters, a game plan will be drawn up for winning with a positive attitude and a sense of humor in the race against despair and insanity. In chapters 6 and 7, you'll learn how to outmaneuver weakness by turning it into strength; and then seek to expose the Ideal Parent as a myth. In chapter 8 you'll learn how to be a good loser, as well as the formula for gracious suffering. Finally, in chapter 9, you'll be introduced to the ultimate strategic weapon for combating guilt and parenting teenagers: *unlimited, unconditional love.*

As we move into the next chapter, I'd like to leave you with a positive thought. Remember the mouse in the elephant's footprint? Well, fortunately, the ground was soft, and it survived.

4

Turn on the Power of Positives

The first strategic maneuver required in becoming a guilt-free parent is a positive attitude. Without it, all the other strategies would probably be ineffective.

Dwell on the positive qualities in yourself and in your children was one of the goals outlined in chapter 3. That goal, of course, is based on the apostle Paul's formula for positive thinking, Philippians 4:8. Paul indicated I should concentrate on ". . . the fine, good things in others."

I really wanted to think positive thoughts about my kids, but I found the assignment harder and harder as they progressed into their middle teens. How could I keep my mind focused on positives, when my sometimes resistant and defiant teenagers kept coming up with negative behavior?

For example, one day during Dave's ninth-grade year, I got a call from the school office to verify Dave's illness. Dave wasn't sick. He'd skipped. My mind went negative.

I THINK POSITIVE UNTIL . . .

This negative thought process had been occurring with increasing frequency since Dave started junior high. I didn't like the feelings. You see, for most things, I'd never had much trouble thinking positively. I have always had a positive attitude about my marriage, my home, my friends, and my cat. In fact, if Ron suddenly announced, "We're moving to Point Barrow, Alaska," I'm sure I could adjust. After a couple days of shock, I'd find *something* good, right, or lovely about the idea.

Look on the bright side, I'd say to myself, *you always did want to drive a dog sled.*

It's true. I have the ability to "bloom *almost* anywhere I'm planted." Consequently, I couldn't understand why my positive thoughts sometimes seemed to vanish when my teenagers were involved. Some days, as when Dave played hooky, I let my imagination wander into all sorts of negative pitfalls. Why had Dave skipped school? Was he into drugs? What if he's run away? And what about Caryl—she hasn't gotten into trouble yet, but, what if. . . . Believe me, with everything teenagers can get into these days, the list was endless.

As usual, I ended up blowing the problem way out of proportion. Before I knew what had happened, my guilt had convinced me, "It's too late now; you blew it. If you'd handled things differently. . . ." If it were up to my guilty conscience, everything that ever happened (and even stuff that didn't) would be my fault.

To further complicate matters, I fell into a tailspin as I thought, not only of what the kids could do to themselves, but what others could do to them. Fear blackened my mind with gloom, as I thought of the terrible tragedies that could overtake my children. I really had to struggle to get my mind back to the realization that no matter what happens to them, God is in control.

And speaking of God's being in control, I decided I'd better do some praying about the negative problem I'd gotten myself into. I'd built up so much more negative than positive over Dave's truancy, I nearly overloaded my system. I needed help and so I prayed:

> Lord, how about showing me ways to concentrate on the positive attributes of my children? Right now my focus is bent on the worst. I know there are good things. It's just that when we're in the middle of an ugly scene, the good fades faster than blue jeans.
>
> Oh . . . and thanks, Lord!

STEP ONE: LIST THEIR POSITIVES

I knew the answer would come and it did. *Why not list the positive character traits of both kids?* So I tried it. It was difficult at first. My brain wasn't used to a positive power struggle. The negative thoughts retaliated in an effort to force back any positive flow. I got so frustrated, I almost turned myself in to the Home for Emotionally Handicapped Mothers of Teenagers. But I persevered and was finally able to consciously take hold of the negatives and turn them around.

As an example, both Dave and Caryl are heavily equipped with *stubbornness.* Dave can argue his way out of any mess (including that school-skipping caper). "It was my first offense," he argued. "Didn't you an' Dad ever skip school?" He's not always right, but his *endurance* is phenomenal, and he wears his opponent down. He can come up with more arguments for his defense than a team of the nation's top ten lawyers. In lawyers, this trait might be termed *persuasive.* There's only one person who can out-talk Dave—his father.

Caryl's stubborn streak turns to *eagerness* or *aggressive endurance* as she participates in her favorite sport, gymnastics. Caryl is *determined* to be a good gymnast, as she pushes herself beyond the pain of blistered hands, aching joints and muscles, and fear of falling.

One of the most aggravating characteristics in Caryl, at least for me, is her snail's pace. It can take this girl up to three days to do a half-hour job. After hours of deliberation, I finally reversed *slowpoke* to *patient, persistent,* and *imaginative.* Don't laugh! It takes a lot of imagination to come up with enough detours to spend one week washing a single load of clothes.

Another of Dave's bad traits is his *strong will.* The strength behind his *will* can, if channeled in the right direction, develop Dave into an *assertive, motivated, dynamic* young man. Sometimes I think only God will be able to subdue and channel Dave's strong will, but my positive thoughts urge me to believe this young man will make it.

Hey! It works! Once I broke the negative power struggle, finding positive traits in my children was as elementary as deciding on the right hat. (Well . . . I never promised you instant success.)

START A "POSITIVE MEMORY" BOOK

As I began finding positive thoughts instead of negative ones to relate to my teenagers, I decided I needed a place to record them for future reference. This led to the development of a journal. I bought one of those "Write Your Own Book" books entitled *One Day at a Time.* An appropriate title, don't you think? In it, I listed all the good, right, and lovely thoughts about my teenagers I could think of. The journal now serves as a positive memory book.

Now, when our teenagers do something exciting, positive, or even antinegative, I write it in the journal. The entries are, so to speak, deposited in the bank account of memories. They are placed in the debit column, like cash on hand—forever saved, because the credits are never deducted. In other words, I try to forget the crummy attitudes and nasties as quickly as possible.

As an example, my son thanked me for making dinner a few nights ago. He did! He actually thanked me.

He said, "Thanks, Mom, for making dinner." Then to add shock to astonishment, he added, "It was good."

"You're welcome," I stammered, staring wide-eyed in amazement at the mouth that usually registered complaints.

I quickly found my *One Day . . .* journal and made my entry.

May 20—Great news! Today Dave thanked me for dinner—he appreciates me.

An exceptional entry. Sometimes a day goes by and all I have entered is: *Dave walked by me in the hall today—without sneering.*

The journal is a book full of pluses. On days when mouthing off, rejecting authority, and just plain orneriness are the order of the day, I can say, "This too will pass." I begin to read the good stuff and I can cope with the discouragement of the moment.

FINDING POSITIVE POWER IN PHOTO ALBUMS

Along with the journal, photo albums prove an excellent source for reviving good times. Seeing life in a positive way is helpful to the kids as well as us parents—especially on days when they tend to be particularly contrary.

Last Saturday, for instance, was a bummer. Every word my teenager uttered offended me. He'd not only gotten up on the wrong side of the bed, he must have slept on it all night. What a grouch!

Positive thought drowned in a sea of negative attitudes.

In urgent desperation, I finally took out the family album and began to page through Dave's childhood memories. I giggled as my eyes wandered from one lively growing-up shot to the next.

Fortunately, his curiosity woke up and won. Together, we became absorbed in positives. His impish grins; first headstand; playing Dr. Doolittle with a giant, stuffed turtle; and standing high in the air on Dad's strong hands, melted the day's hostility.

As we watched, a little boy grew up, happy in the captured moments of time.

Happiness is not always the outcome of a lousy day. I've known times of pessimistic despair. Times when I'd curl up alone in the 2:00 A.M. darkness of an all-night vigil wondering, "Why? Where did I go wrong?"

At times like that, I must turn from the negative and come to play the positive game alone. While I read my journal, tears wash my cheeks. I remember. . . . He was okay then; he'll be okay again.

A verse from Psalms heads my journal. ". . . Weeping may tarry for the night, but joy comes with the morning" (30:5).

DON'T IGNORE YOUR EMOTIONS

As you grow toward being a positive parent, you can count on opposition. Everytime a negative thought creeps in, guilt may chase you with feelings such as, "You're supposed to think positive, sadness is negative—you've failed!"

Along with guilt comes fear and worry, which will continue to confuse you with such thoughts as, "This is no time to think positive. What kind of parent are you? This is the time to worry, worry, worry!"

To make matters worse, anxiety nibbles away on your tender stomach lining, teasing, "Good Christians don't get ulcers. If positive thinking settles the stomach, what happened to you?"

Don't let your overactive emotional imagination get you down. Remember, positive thinking doesn't mean wearing a permanent smile or jumping for joy every minute of the day. Positive thinking is more like accepting your God-given emotions of anger, grief, concern, and tears. Let go! Express these emotions. Then know they will bring you back to the realization of how much we all need God. And, that's *positive!*

Positive thinking is relying on God's promises; to "know that in everything God works for good with those who love him . . ." (Romans 8:28).

Positive thinking is trusting God for the future of your children and knowing only He can bring it about—His way.

A positive thinker asks these questions: "How can the tragedy of a rebellious child bring me closer to God?" and, "How will God use this trial in my life to make me a better, more useful person?"

FORMULA FOR POSITIVE THINKING

If you are asking, "How can I implement a positive-thinking theory in my life?" here are some suggestions.

When we are faced with problems, our minds look for solutions. Unfortunately, all too often, the negatives seem to outweigh the positives. But, there is a way to change all that.

Learn to recognize your negative thoughts when they surface. Say to yourself, "This thought is negative; I need something positive." At first it may take a while for your brain to respond, but keep trying. Search and pray—positive thoughts will come.

Consider this formula for positive thinking:

Negative equals Minus (−); Positive equals Plus (+).

With a (−) you subtract or take away from yourself. If you were to flourish your negative (−) with a couple of periods, you'd get a divider (÷). With negatives, whether you subtract or divide, you always end up with less than you had before.

On the other hand, with a (+) you can add. Add a measure of fullness to your life. If you tilt the positive (+) slightly to the left or right, you have a multiplier (×). With positives, you can multiply yourself into a richer, more rewarding, and happier life.

Suppose, for example, your family started the day wallowing in a pit of negativism. It happened to me the other morning. I was brutally awakened at 7:00 A.M. by shouting in the hallway, just outside my bedroom door.

"Shut up!" yelled Dave. I plugged my ears and rolled over. (−1)

"You jerk!" Caryl screeched, as if to insure against my sleeping in. (−2)

I pulled the covers over my head to muffle the hostile sounds. Unfortunately, Ron's louder and closer voice joined the chorus of negatives as he boomed in my ears, "Can't you guys stop arguing for five minutes? You're driving me nuts!" (−3)

Further sleep had become as much a possibility as bagging a Bengal tiger in my living room. *Now,* I said to myself, *you can either come out fighting or smiling.* I chose to smile, as I kissed my husband and glided out the bedroom door and down the hall. "Good morning!" I greeted, and gave each kid a hug. "What would you like for breakfast?" (+1, 2, and 3)

"What's so good about it?" Dave jeered. (−4)

"What're you so happy about?" Caryl sneered. "Can't you get rid of that creep. I was in the bathroom first and he comes along and shoves me out." (−5 and 6)

"Hey, little sister, butt out. I have to get ready first. *I* take priority." (−7)

"Time!" I shouted. Is it too late for positives? Has the Rushford family divided itself asunder? *Never!* (At least not as long as I have positive power.) "What do you want for breakfast?" I repeated with a grin. (+4)

"Bacon, eggs, hashbrowns, toast, and hot chocolate," bellowed the husky voice from the male-dominated bathroom.

"Pancakes," Caryl injected.

"It's as good as done." (+5)

"How come you're being so nice?" they asked in unison.

"Do you want I should yell? Three grouches is enough for one morning. Besides, the day goes better when you start happy." I threw out a few more pluses of praise to even the score. By the time the kids left for school, positives had multiplied into three happy faces. A few minutes later Ron's added one more plus. (Final score, Minuses −7; Pluses +11.)

There's plus power in a positive parent. You can have an influence over the negatives that work to divide your family. Start by recognizing your negatives. Determine to turn them into positives by adding a vertical line for strength. (−) plus (|) equals (+). Now imagine this vertical line connecting you and God, because it's God who makes it possible to build pluses out of minuses. The process takes time, but it can be done. I'm told it takes twenty-one days to form a habit. So, think positively. Concentrate. Pray. Tomorrow you'll have only twenty days to go.

SIX STEPS TO A POSITIVELY POWERFUL PARENT

1. Make a list of positive attributes in yourself, your spouse (if married), and your children.

2. Tuck these lists in a convenient place, like your Bible, journal, or family album. Look at them everyday for twenty-one days of habit forming.

3. Make a list of Bible verses or familiar quotes that add plus power to your thinking. Refer to at least one or two of these per day.

4. Be assured in your heart that even if you feel negative for a while—as much as a day or two—it won't last forever. (Even if you've been negative for years, there's hope.)

5. After the twenty-one days, keep these lists and verses in an easy-to-get-to-place for reference when you feel yukky or when someone puts you in the pits.

6. Pray. In order to succeed to the realm of Powerful Parent, you'll need to draw daily from our all-powerful God.

5

Loosen Up and Laugh

Equally close in character to a positive attitude comes the ability to find joy in all things. You'll find that it is possible to find joy or humor in life situations, ourselves, and even in our teenagers.

One of our goals as parents, seeking to survive the problems inherent in raising teenagers, is to "rejoice always." "An impossible task," you say? You may be right, but maybe we can learn to rejoice always—at least part of the time.

HOW CAN YOU LAUGH AT A TRAGEDY?

"Rejoice? A sense of humor?" Janet, a close friend, complained. "How do you expect me to laugh? All life to our fifteen-year-old, Kim, is a continual rerun of *Macbeth.* There is no neutral ground. Tears, anger, and resentment pour out at a moment's notice. If I happen to catch an accidental grin, she turns it off faster than a chipmunk scurries into a burrow. Life for Kim is a series of tragedies. A broken date equals the end of the world."

For Kim, as well as many other teenagers, life is an explosive chain of crises. Their limited experience with living hasn't taught them that, in spite of turmoil, trauma, and broken hearts, life goes on. They have yet to learn how to shed tears, nurture and heal their wounds, then return to the world and business as usual.

Our children haven't learned to laugh at life and at their mistakes. If we parents take our teenagers' dramatics too seriously, our lives end up as catastrophic as the television soaps. Children need parents who don't disintegrate. They need parents who can see beyond the moment's devastated ruins; someone to assure them that there is life after a broken date, a lost notebook, or a parental *no.*

This assurance should be made, not by laughing at them or teasing them about their seriousness, but by example. We set this example as we maintain our own sense of humor and come out on top of our own problems with a smile and an inner peace.

REJOICE ... ALWAYS?

Surviving the dramatic circumstances encountered while rearing teenagers is like trying to swim in split pea soup. The more we struggle, the deeper we sink. Regardless of how difficult a situation seems, the Scriptures tell us, "Rejoice in the Lord always; again I will say, Rejoice" (Philippians 4:4).

I struggled with that verse for a long time—had some long and tedious guilt trips too. Questions permeated my mind. What does God mean—*rejoice always?* How is it possible?

The revelation took place when Dave was fourteen and Caryl, twelve. My grandmother had just died. It was through her death that I finally began to realize a person could, indeed, find joy in every situation.

Although I grieved for the loss of her life, I was able to rejoice in her final release. "Rejoice always" finally made sense. Rejoicing always is possible, but only through God. For me, as an imperfect human, continual joy and happiness is impossible. I experience pain, tears, remorse, and despair; but in Christ, a part of me (through the Holy Spirit) always rejoices. Through Christ and His promises, I know God will work for the good, and joy is always present; even when I don't *feel* it.

To rejoice takes concentrated effort. I try to find a reason or beneficial outcome for everything. True, this philosophy hasn't and won't bring an end to life's problems, but they are a lot easier to bear.

Let's face it, many experiences, especially those concerning our children, are no laughing matter. In time, though, we may be able to see the good, the lessons learned, how we grew and benefited from the experiences. Meanwhile, find humor when you can as you "Rejoice in the Lord always."

LAUGHTER IS STILL THE BEST MEDICINE

I love to laugh, and to see my kids laugh fills me up. I bubble over with delight. Laughter brightens our home like a million Christmas lights. We find sport in outdoing each other in wit.

The other day, my husband, Ron, qualified for Wit of the Week. Dave had taken up residence in his favorite spot in the kitchen one evening after dinner. While I cleaned up the dishes, he sat on a stool at the counter with the telephone receiver clutched securely to the side of his face. The inarticulate murmurs transmitted through to his peer at the other end of the connection made me wonder if maybe teenagers had worked out a secret code. I stood within two feet of him and couldn't understand a word he said.

Ron entered. Dave's mumbling stopped. I felt sorry for the person on the other end of the line; but the kid probably knew exactly what was going on.

"Honey!" Ron exclaimed. "I think we're going to have to consider surgery for our son."

"What?"

"Yes. He's got this big white growth on the side of his face. It's been there so long, I'm afraid he'll need an amputation."

"Dumb," our teenager retorted. He held back a grin.

Laughter bounced around the walls of our small, efficient kitchen. A giggle inadvertently slipped out of our normally solemn-faced son, then a wide smile.

"I'm sure," he added as he stifled his smile and laughter into a dignified, somber tone. But he couldn't fool us. The light still twinkled in his eyes.

Score another one for Ron. He has the gift of finding humor in almost everything. You'll find humor, smiles, giggles, and uncontrolled laughter are as contagious as chicken pox. Beware! If allowed in your home, they spread.

Aside from its contagious qualities, laughter is medicinal. We find it relieves anxiety and frustration, and makes life more enjoyable. To laugh until the tears flow is an exciting and exhausting remedy for tension.

CAUTION: HANDLE LAUGHTER WITH CARE

Care should be taken, however, that we don't make fun of our children. Teasing can be dangerous from the wrong mouth. Not all kids can handle it. Safety lies in laughing at ourselves, our feelings, and problems. Gently search out the key to unlock the humor in your child. Each teenager is different so HANDLE WITH CARE and PROCEED WITH CAUTION.

Everyday situations can be extremely volatile for the teenager. As adults, we can teach our kids that tragedies of today don't necessarily mean the end of life. Sometimes we can use humor as a tool; sometimes we can't.

For example, I would have been cruel to laugh at or tease my daughter about the shoes she wanted for a school dance. I'd be wrong to belittle her strong emotions.

"If I can't have high heels for the dance, I'll just die." (Compared to the negative reaction Caryl fears from her peers, dying looks good.)

Timing and consideration of feelings is all-important. Sometimes I miss the seriousness of a problem. I've been known to push the laugh button too soon, or embarrass one of my kids in an attempt to be funny. For instance, when Caryl (undeveloped at thirteen) asked me for a training bra, and I retorted with, "Training for what?" She didn't laugh.

At times like that I have to say, "I'm sorry."

They usually come back with a grin or, "It's okay Mom." Apologies accepted. They know I'm human. I make mistakes. Most of the time, though, laughter wins.

KIDS CAN BE COMEDIANS TOO

My children are not without their own sense of humor. As a teenager, Dave would have us believe humor is beneath him. Caryl, on the other hand, still loves to outwit her dad and me.

Old stoneface Dave cracks up when I remind him of his first naughty words: *dirty water*. And, he can't resist a grin when I tell him about the time he embarrassed me royally when he was three.

We were caught in a bustling Christmas crowd, and to make better time, I picked Dave up and carried him. Just then a small, squeaky voice behind me cried, "Help! Help!" I turned—saw nothing and continued walking. The tiny voice cried again, "Help! Help!" I turned around.

One lady frowned at me. A man looked at me suspiciously. My adrenalin jumped 80 percent, as I realized the furry-jacketed bundle I carried had been calling to the crowd behind us, pretending I'd taken him captive. At being discovered, he giggled mercilessly. He then took on the appearance of the youngest member of the Vienna Boys' Choir. His red-faced, bewildered mother saw little humor in the situation until later. But, it didn't take me too long to catch the hilarity in my three-year-old son's mischievous actions.

Everybody, especially parents, needs a good sense of humor. Can you imagine life without laughter? There are numerous fun games suitable for teenagers and parents, but whether you choose to play games or pick up on humorous incidents, the idea is to work on developing a good sense of humor. Humor is a valuable and indispensable commodity. Fill your house, whenever you can, with the joy of it. Bear in mind, however, that although humor is not always possible—*rejoicing always* is.

As we strive to develop joyfulness, we can be certain that Satan will be constantly on guard to convince us of the impossibility of finding joy in all things. Don't be deceived. Remember, like a positive attitude, rejoicing doesn't depend on how you feel, but rather, your relationship toward God.

Rejoicing always means finding *joy* in all of God's creations: from a small pebble on the beach to a rainbow with color reaching from one end of the sky to the other; or from Bach to a teenager playing rock.

Joy is reading a book or finding a flower in the desert.

Joy is hearing your children say, "I love you," or getting a return hug, or just hearing them say, "Hi!" And sometimes *joy* can be getting a phone call from your runaway son who says, "Mom, Dad, I'm coming home." But, *joy* can be just knowing he's okay, even if he isn't coming home.

Remember, total joy is available only through close fellowship with Christ. Let His Holy Spirit fill you up and overflow you with lasting joy to help you meet the sorrows of the world.

DOS AND DON'TS FOR HUMOR IN YOUR HOME

1. Even if your teenager won't laugh or crack a smile, keep smiling anyway. You will bring a sense of happiness and security to his or her overturned world.

2. Parents teach by example. Sullenness and depression are as addicting as wit, winsomeness, and joy. Be a humor pusher, not a frown maker.

3. It never hurts to stash a couple of squirt guns for an emergency to wash away scowls. One of the pediatricians in the clinic where I work carries just such a weapon. He uses it to wet down the blues and lift up laughter and lighten the work load.

4. Write the words *Let Loose and Laugh* on a paper. Tape it to the fridge as a reminder of the new, winsome, and wonderful you.

5. Keep telling yourself, "I'd rather have laugh lines than wrinkles."

6. If frolicking isn't your game, be content with optimism. Express encouragement to yourself and those around you.

7. Act natural. Accept the fact that you're not Phyllis Diller, Red Skelton, or Erma Bombeck, unless, of course, you are. Be yourself. Let humor come in its own time. Just as you wouldn't make yourself cry all day, you wouldn't want to force humor either. Humor is best, like tears, when neither suppressed or forced.

8. Make Beethoven's "Ode to Joy" your theme song. It will inspire you.

9. Pray for the peace of God to give you cause to *rejoice*. Whether daily or hourly, look to God for reinforcement.

6

Turn Your Weakness Into Strength

How are you doing? Have you started laughing yet? Still crying? I hope by now, you've begun to feel good about yourself and your job as a parent. Are you looking at roses—or do you still have your eyes on thorns?

Have patience. Hardly anyone calls positive thinking and the ability to rejoice easy. (But then some people would say raising teenagers is easy.) If you've been up half the night wondering, "What could Jennifer be doing at this hour?" and shudder to think about it—I understand. If you've spent the afternoon crying, because you and your son got into a name-calling, blame-placing fight—you're forgiven. Nobody's perfect. Besides, we're not finished yet.

In order to master the emotionalism brought on by my emerging teenagers, I continued to try to perfect my six essential strategies. In the last two chapters I shared on how to develop a positive attitude and gain the ability to rejoice in all things. Now let's share the secrets of parental strength. That doesn't mean I'm going to bounce out of a phone booth with a background chorus singing "Supermom!" I don't even own a cape. In fact, sometimes I feel about as strong as a guppy in a school of sharks. Such was the case one day last summer.

THE CASE OF THE TOO-SHORT SWIMSUIT

Dave and Caryl were trying to manipulate me, and they were succeeding. They certainly picked a good day for the attack. It was 102 degrees in the shade and at least 95 degrees in my office. They timed their invasion with the precision of a Green Beret platoon.

"Mom, I need a blank check for a new swimsuit," Caryl advised.

"But I just bought you one last month."

"It's too short."

"That's impossible. What did you do, buy it too small?"

"I'm sure, Mom. I purposely got the suit too small so you'd have to buy me a new one," Caryl remarked sarcastically. "The dumb thing falls off when I dive."

"Don't dive." (The thought of buying another swimsuit in mid-August panicked me. Our teen-eaten budget would surely collapse under the strain.)

"Mom, I'm taking the moped to Shawn's to go swimming." Dave threw his distracting voice up the stairwell.

"No! You don't have a helmet."

"What's a helmet got to do with buying me a swimsuit?" Caryl complained from the living room.

"Not you, Caryl."

"That's stupid," Dave snarled.

"You always pay more attention to David than you do to me," Caryl pouted. "How am I supposed to go swimming?"

"Oh . . . well . . . I suppose. . . ."

"Thanks, Mom. Bye!" came a booming voice from the garage. Before I could yell my objection, he'd zipped down the street and out of earshot.

Rats! I lost! How's a parent to remain a pillar of strength when faced with a strategic move like that? I felt more like Napoleon at Waterloo.

A couple of Olive Oyl arms wrapped around me from behind, while soft lips brushed my cheek. "Thanks, Mom. I knew you'd understand."

I left my typewriter and, like a prisoner of war, trudged after my daughter to the oven-hot car. Obediently, I followed her in and out of sporting-goods stores and finally into an air-conditioned mall. There, I regained my composure and dignity, as the cool atmosphere revitalized my limp, shopworn body.

Caryl found her new swimsuit. And, thanks to a clearance sale, the nine-dollar price and our budget proved compatible. The final score: Kids 3, Parent 1. It wasn't a total loss. After all, one of my *teenagers* hugged *me.*

HOW CAN YOU BE STRONG WHEN YOU'RE WEAK?

As the above illustration clearly shows, my kids have become pros at manipulating me. How about you? Have your kids ever worked you until you felt like a weak, shapeless wad of clay? Teenagers, especially when you're dealing with two or more, have an uncanny ability to keep you off balance. I usually feel like I'm a step or two behind—and never quite in control of the situation.

So, in light of all this, how does a parent become strong? Is it possible to reach up out of this weakness and find any strength at all? After some serious thought, I came up with several ways to regain and maintain strength—even in my weaker moments.

The first step is to admit my weakness. It takes strength to admit it when they get the best of me. After all, one failure out of ten isn't bad. (Just between us, sometimes the stats are lower.)

A second step is to realize that there is more to being a strong parent than muscle and complete control.

Developing strength as a parent has been difficult for me. During my early twenties, I didn't know how to rear a defiant child without the excruciating pang of guilt sinking deep into my inexperienced feelings. Dave was always in trouble and in need of a strong hand—in the right place. Which brings us to (you guessed it) the "strong-willed child."

For me, James Dobson and his taming of *The Strong-Willed Child* came too late. He did, however, make me feel better about myself as a parent. He helped me realize I did all right, in spite of the possible pitfalls encountered in raising one of those plentiful species. I recommend Dr. Dobson's book for anyone who has trouble understanding how one child in the family can cause more trouble in a day than ten others in their entire lifetimes.

My strong-willed child became my stronger-willed teenager, and the trouble doubled. When God passed around wills, Dave thought He said *bills* and stockpiled in case of depression.

For a while, I thought brute strength and determination were all we needed to keep our son in line. But, unfortunately, he grew. This growth brought about the burning question, "Can there be strength without muscle?"

How do I get my teenager to do what I think is best for him without using physical strength? Not that muscle is possible. A mother like me (all five feet-two inches) is in no position to use a deltoid muscle as a weapon. I haven't beat Dave at arm wrestling since he became fifteen. (I still throw a good bluff, though, so don't blow my cover.)

In all honesty, I realized the physical strength of a parent only reigned until my kids grew bigger than I. Then I encountered the frustrating, get-nowhere battle of wills.

Therefore, I have come to the conclusion that the parent must be stronger in ways other than physical when dealing with strong-willed children, especially during their teenage years. The answer is to become *The Strong-Willed Parent.*

Not a bad idea, but how can a softy like me pull it off?

GOD—THE STRONG-WILLED PARENT

I decided the best way to learn was by using a role model. The best example of a strong-willed parent is God. Of course, He is my ultimate source of strength and authority on parenting. I fully recommend a few sessions with Him, and some extensive study in His Book if you find yourself a weak, ineffective parent. I was exactly that. As I mentioned before, I've spent a great deal of time talking to God about my problems, and finding strength to cope with my teenagers was no exception. In one of these conversations with God, I had a great revelation—one that could practically cancel parental guilt. Naturally, with a decrease in guilt, I could see an increase in strength.

"Lord, I haven't the strength to be a parent," I declared one day after a Teenager −10, Parent −0 loss. "I need help! Can there be strength without muscle? If so, I could use some right now."

I thought for a moment about God's position as Father. I notice He doesn't use much muscle these days. Ever since the Flood, He's been sort of laid back. Except for a few exceptions, He's shown remarkable restraint. He seldom reaches down to physically whack His children anymore. His approach of late is more subtle, but He certainly has a way of commanding respect. He lays down the law—we obey, or else. There are quite a few of God's children who fall into the "or else" category—much to God's dismay. Our Father gives us knowledge and expects us to make the right choices. So I went on:

> Lord, You are strong and expect Your children to obey. When we don't, You let us know, so that we can confess and get right with You. Your grace is more than fair. However, it has come to my attention that You too have your share of rebellious children. But Lord, You are the *perfect* parent. Does this mean rebellious children are not necessarily a sign of weakness?

What a breakthrough! If parents blame a child's rebellion on themselves, they would ultimately have to consider God responsible for the rebellious acts of all people. How foolish! Each person is accountable for his or her own acts.

REBELLION—WHO'S RESPONSIBLE?

This is *good news.* It is insight which substantially reduced my guilt feelings—at least temporarily. Parents don't need to feel guilt, worry, anxiety, or fear over our children's decision to rebel. The child is responsible.

Hmmm. . . . I could feel guilt creeping in already, as my inner interrogation committee threw out questions. Responsible, yes, but at what age? Are you sure? The child is still a minor. If only I hadn't. . . .

Hold it! I had a positive theory going, and here comes Satan and my psychological guilt complex, trying to overload my emotional circuit. I decided to deal with each question one at a time. This time I refused to be subterfuged with confusion.

First, *at what age* is the child accountable? A tough question. I guess I'd have to say, the age at which they make the decision to establish their own life-style—"do their own thing," whether that life-style is contrary to or corresponding with the beliefs and desires of their parents. I have concluded that for our home, at seventeen, our son, David, is responsible for his own behavior. His defiant acts are his alone.

With the first question firmly settled in my mind, I tackled the next. "What are *my* responsibilities in getting Dave grown up and out on his own? After all, he's still a minor, and here I am with little or no control. I can't force him to obey."

Because our physical strength is greatly impaired as our children grow older, parents have no choice but to resort to the strength they have left—inner strength. Ron and I can counsel our kids, love them, and pray for them. We can set down rules and expect those rules to be followed. And, if they aren't followed, our teenagers will be subject to logical consequences.

THE POWER OF LOGICAL CONSEQUENCES

Since they are responsible for their actions, our sons and daughters must face the logical consequences of their deeds. As parents, we often set up those logical consequences as we follow through and sternly uphold our home rules. There are instances, however, when a broken rule or law calls for measures beyond our control. Sometimes authorities must be called in to administer justice. (Read Bruce Narramore's views in *Adolescence Is Not an Illness* for his treatment of the logical consequences.)

One of the most difficult acts a parent performs is one of consequential punishment, especially when it involves police intervention.

Carla, a close friend, and her husband, Paul, found themselves facing this dilemma. A school counselor advised them that their fourteen-year-old, Christie, had been smoking pot at school. "I think you ought to authorize Juvenile to pick her up."

"Why are you calling me?" questioned Carla. "Why didn't you call the police?"

"To tell the truth, I'm breaking a confidence by letting you know. But, I like Christie. She's a good kid, and I don't want to see her get into any more trouble."

"I could never have her picked up. I don't want my little girl in jail, not for a minute."

"Christie's breaking the law. A head-on collision with the authorities could scare her enough to set her straight. She knows you wouldn't turn her in. A strong action on your part would let her know you mean business. If you really love Christie, you'll take care of the problem now."

Carla and Paul reluctantly followed the counselor's advice and remain grateful to him. Although their problems with Christie didn't end abruptly, she knew her parents would take any action necessary to keep her in line.

It takes a special kind of strength called courage to stand your ground, enforce rules, and maintain authority. When you love your children, you use all the power available—physical, emotional, and mental, to keep them from ruining their lives. It's called parental love with a strong backing.

THE "TOUGHLOVE" APPROACH

"Getting Tough With Teens" is the title of an article published in *Time* Magazine (June 8, 1981). The article disclosed a fairly new and successful association called "Toughlove."

"Toughlove" was founded by a couple, David and Phyllis York, when they realized being Mr. and Mrs. Nice Guy to their teenagers wasn't working. The organization is made up of ". . . anxious parents who were dedicated to drawing the line against out-of-control youngsters and forcing them to behave." The article goes on to explain, "Toughlove parents are encouraged to 'set the bottom line' on acceptable behavior and back it up by forbidding use of the family car, limiting phone calls, and refusing to intervene when a youngster is in trouble."

I suppose that approach sounds drastic. It does to me, but I look at it this way: if I don't do everything in my power or strength to keep the kids straight, Satan will push my sensitive emotions to enormous proportions. I'd be barraged with *if onlys.*

"If only I'd been firm."

"If only I'd taken the car keys."

"If only I'd punished him the first time."

"If only . . ." and the list goes on and on. All I need in my life is more guilt. Sorry, but I for one am not giving Satan any more freedom than he already has. Consequently, I'll do anything short of handcuffing my kid to his bed, locking the bedroom, and shoving meals under the door until he's twenty-one, to keep him out of trouble.

Like anything else, Toughlove may not work for everyone. While getting tough might be a comfortable solution for some parents, others may want to try an alternate program. The method itself is not the issue. The key to your strength is to do the best job possible for you, in your style of parenting, and leave the rest to God.

For any situation, whether mildly tense or extremely difficult, my job as a parent is to muster up all available strength, add a measure from God, and continue to love, counsel, and pray. Just as God gives me the ability to make the best of a bad situation, He gives me the potential to find strength in my weaknesses.

GOD MAKES ME STRONG

During those tense and trying times, I look to God for help and I pray.

Lord, sometimes I feel helpless to cope with my teenagers and their wrong-way turns. I want to counsel and direct them Your way. I'm not weak because I want to be. It's just that I feel powerless in this self-perpetuating, humanistic society that drives my children away from our morals and values.

Lord, You are the source of strength; I am the shadow of weakness. Today I'm not sure I can continue to fight the battles of a parent. I'd like to turn in my parent badge. I'm not really qualified for the job anyway. You know, I've never been the parent of a teenager before—no prior experience. Would You accept my resignation?

Okay! Okay! You don't need to get pushy about it. I won't give up. I guess kids need parents—even inexperienced ones. Parents, more than ever, need You, Lord.

There is a promise in the Bible: "My grace is sufficient for thee: for my strength is made perfect in weakness ... (2 Corinthians 12:9 KJV).

Lord, I am weak. I look to You for strength.

To gain strength and maintain parental control may be difficult—and maybe even dangerous. Many problems leave me feeling boxed in a canyon where there's no way out but *up.*

STRONG THOUGHTS FOR TIRED PARENTS

God is our strong ally. He invites us to look to Him for strength. Just in case fear emerges with a "You can't make it" philosophy, I have listed a few strong weapons below. Look to these words when weakness and fear threaten to wipe you out:

. . . I will trust, and will not be afraid; for the Lord God is my strength. . . .

Isaiah 12:2

... If God is for us, who is against us?

Romans 8:31

The Lord is my Helper and I am not afraid of anything mere man [or teenager] can do to me.

Hebrews 13:6 TLB

God is our refuge and strength, a very present help in trouble.

Psalms 46:1 KJV

I can do all things in him who strengthens me.

Philippians 4:13

Finally, be strong in the Lord and in the strength of his might.

Ephesians 6:10

As you can see, parents are made strong by a great and powerful God, who will help us overcome the trials and tribulations we encounter during our years of rearing teenagers.

In bringing this strategy for the development of strength to completion, I'd like to recap what it means to be strong.

- *Strong* is parents united with God to regain and maintain authority over our children.

- *Strong* is reliance on God for power to continue life when your child has taken leave without a how or where. He's only said, "It's something I have to do."

- *Strong* is accepting the pain of a child's rebellion and knowing God will win.

- *Strong* is standing firm in your Christian principles amidst ridicule and persecution, while you do what you think is best.

- *Strong* is discipline in love, even if it means rejection.

- *Strong* is to forgive.

- *Strong* is bonding yourself to God in faith and trust.

To paraphrase Paul's conclusion on weakness in 2 Corinthians 12:9, 10, I'll be glad to tell you how weak *I* am, so Christ's power can be demonstrated in me. As a parent of teenagers, I often find myself weakened, insulted, persecuted, and overrun with calamities. Because Christ is my strength, I am content in my dilapidated condition, "for when I am weak, then I am strong."

HOW TO FIND STRENGTH AND INFLUENCE YOUR KIDS

1. What to do when you lose a match of wills.
   a. Accept the loss. Remember, you can't always be a winner.
   b. Forgive yourself.
   c. Think about how you might handle matters differently the next time around.
   d. Remember, when you can accept defeat and love yourself and your kids anyway—you win.

2. What to do to let your teenagers know what you expect of them.
   a. Discuss responsibilities, rules, and logical consequences.
   b. Try a written contract, which can minimize communication problems.
   c. Follow through. Be willing to allow the logical consequences of life to discipline your child—even if it means intervention by "authorities."

3. What to do if you feel your son or daughter is out of control.
   a. Seek outside help from a friend, pastor, or counselor. Don't try to stand alone. Remember, "Two are better than one," and "A threefold cord is not quickly broken."
   b. Contact your pastor or local parish. Find out if there is an active support group for parents. If not, ask if there are other hurting parents within the congregation. Think about the possibility of starting your own prayer or support group.

   c. Write to "Toughlove" for more information on handling
      the teenager in crisis situations. The address is:

> Toughlove
> Community Service Foundation
> P.O. Box 70
> Sellersville, PA 18960

4. Pray daily. Thank and praise God for the strength He gives
you. Trust in His promises to sustain you.

7

Be Real—Not Ideal

A strategy all parents need to develop in dealing with teen-agers is openness, or the ability to be real. As I gained strength to maneuver inch by inch through the minefields of my parent-teenager conflict, I found it necessary to remind myself, "I'm only human," and every parent blows it at times. Even with this philosophy in mind, a large portion of my guilt was caused by the desire to do a *perfect job* of parenting.

Fortunately, life with teenagers soon teaches us how foolish we are to try to cover up our weaknesses. These kids, especially when they're bent on doing things their way, have a way of crumbling the facade of the so-called ideal parent. Yet, too many parents hang tight to the myth of the model parent and end up looking phony.

A KID NEEDS A PARENT, NOT A PAL

For example, some parents try to remain forever young as a means of maintaining communication with their teenagers (or perhaps they're trying to grasp the brass ring of eternal youth).

I met a mother recently, who acted and dressed like her teenage daughter. She tried to be a friend and ended up an enemy—in competition.

Then there's the father who wanted his son to appreciate him. He took him to an *R* rated movie. Since the boy couldn't get in alone, obviously, the father was good for something.

There are parents who practically fall all over themselves, trying desperately to be "one of the gang." Personally, I'm satisfied being a parent. I enjoy cultivating friendships with my children and their friends, as long as they can accept me as I am, an adult parent who loves them and has authority over them.

IDEAL ISN'T REAL

Even more foolish than the adult trying to be a peer is the parent who tries to appear perfect and without blemish. The so-called ideal or model parent is one who relays messages such as:

- "I don't allow my children to see my emotions."

- "We have no problems. We learned early how to speak their language and communicate effectively."

- "We never argue.'·

- "What is a rebellious teenager? We never had one."

- "Our children would never. . . ."

Churchgoing families often take on the appearance of the ideal family. Outwardly saints—inwardly, who knows? At church or when someone calls, it's "Places everyone. Masks up." The stage is set—perfect people in perfect position. Funny thing, I only knew one family I thought was close to perfect— the parents just got a divorce.

It's hard to talk with an ideal parent. As he or she spouts off about their flawless life at home, I can't help wonder, "What is home really like?" I'm sure they must suffer along with the rest of us.

After all, home is where the masks come off, where life is reality. Home is where relationships are authentic, painful, and honest. No acting, no pretense, no facade—only transparent people who openly display their feelings.

A pastor once said of a home he visited, "Everyone was so quiet. The most peaceful place I'd ever seen. Then I noticed why. The relationships were so strained, they weren't even speaking to each other."

In picture-perfect families, when teenagers blow their image and do something stupid, the parents have twice the devastation as we faulty folks. They not only endure the pain suffered for the love of the kids, they also face the embarrassment and the possibility of rejection, when others find them out.

Their cry is often, "How could you *do* this to us?"

"We've failed," they wail. "We've *tried* to be good Christian parents. What will our friends think?"

The parents hammer guilt into the children, and the concept of ideal parenting creates more guilt in the parents. To top it all off, the jig is up. The whole world knows what they *really* are—human! Just like the rest of us—human and authentic— with the capacity to make errors—with the possibility of failure.

Authenticity is being open and real with each other. It's being transparent or letting your feelings show through without shame. Feelings of love, fear, sorrow, and happiness. Authenticity is honesty.

I PLANNED A PERFECT FAMILY BUT ...

There are many times when I don't particularly like being authentic. Times when I would rather hide behind a mask of perfection. Since we're being open and honest, I'll have to confess that I did wear a mask for many years. It took a long while before I could admit my failures as a parent openly. After all, I had the perfect family: a handsome husband; a boy first; then two years later, a girl. They were blue-eyed, blond, and beautiful. Perfect! Right?

Wrong. Problems seeped into our model family. At first I thought we were abnormal. If only I'd been able to confess my uglies to others, I'd have saved myself mountains of anguish.

When I finally heard the words of other mothers and fathers, sharing their miseries and their raw spots in dealing with teenagers, I decided to come clean. It wasn't easy, and it took some time, but I realized that life is better when you are real. To prepare for my new role as a "nonperfect parent," I read the Bible and talked to God—a lot:

> God, all this talk about being real, being authentic and transparent, frightens me. Will people still like me when they know the *real* me? When they see how weak and vulnerable I can be ... do You think they'll want to associate with me?
>
> You know I'm not looking for sympathy, Lord. It's just ... I'm tired of playing make-believe games. I'm sick of smiling and insisting everything is great, when it's not. Sometimes I'm really hurting inside and could use a friend who understands. If I am honest and say how I truly feel, will I still be alone?

Even though the Bible reassured me that everyone sinned and no one, not even one, could claim perfection (Romans 3:23) and that "... there is nothing new under the sun" (Ecclesiastes 1:9), my uncertainty still reigned:

> But, Lord, what about the times I felt so miserably unhappy, I wanted to walk out the door—leave my husband, my

children and . . . everything. If I told someone that . . . I don't know. I'm afraid they'd stare blankly at me or say, "How could anyone who calls herself a Christian be capable of uttering such nonsense?"

Still, the words of God echoed in my mind. "Therefore, putting away falsehood, let every one speak the truth with his neighbor, for we are members one of another" (Ephesians 4:25).

Be real? Be truthful? I just couldn't, Lord. Why if our friends and neighbors knew about some of the fights we've had, I'll bet they'd never speak to us.

And so, I argued with God, knowing all the while I would come to be real—eventually. I even went so far as to try to talk God into making the task easier for me.

Lord, if You were to guarantee me that people would be understanding, kind, and honest in return, I'd be more than happy to. . . .

But, I knew He wouldn't guarantee what anyone would say or do. I would have to chance it. No—better yet—I would have to *step out in faith.*

I WANTED TO BE REAL, BUT . . .

You may be wondering why being honest and authentic was so important to me. I had seen the path taken by *real* people and the one trod by *pretend* people. I knew which path I had to choose. People who were real and open with me helped me recognize that I wasn't abnormal, my feelings weren't strange or inhuman. Those who pretended made me feel guilty and inadequate. I was willing to take the chance of being hurt, if, by sharing, I could help even one person.

Even though I knew how useful sharing could be, fear gripped my throat everytime I tried to speak out. I got choked up and knew that if and when the words did emerge, I'd cry. The source of strength I needed to overcome my fears would have to come from God.

> Lord, I'm convinced truthfulness and authenticity are right for me, but I need Your help to succeed. Bind my fears, so I can tell people who I really am. So I can admit, "Hey! Over here! It's me. A parent who argues with her kids, who has temper tantrums, and who sometimes gets hostile. A mother who cries and laughs . . . I'm real."
>
> Oh, and Lord, it's okay to share the good stuff too, isn't it? I'd hate to have people think I'm all bad. Thanks, Lord.

In practicing my newly acquired authenticity, I decided home was the best place for a practice run. My children would see the real me—not that they didn't have a pretty good idea already, but I had been keeping a few feelings from them.

Being honest with my children means showing them more than a flash of anger. They need to know that when they hurt me I cry, and when they tickle me, I laugh. When they do special things, like win an award, get an *A* or *B* or even bring a *D* up to a *C,* I am joyful and proud. When they hurt, I hurt. I tell them of my concern and let them know I pray for them, and if they want, we pray together.

With all this honesty, we remain far from perfect. That only happens in the movies, or on the surface. We still fight, feel resentment, anger, and jealousy. We make mistakes; but God loves us anyway. God even helps us love each other. Even with all our impurities, our humanity, we are loved.

Authenticity becomes a bit more difficult to attain as we move beyond the family relationships. Yet, it is a priority in establishing sharing relationships with other parents. In order to support those who are in the middle of struggles and trials, you need to be able to admit your own faults and problems. As I have said before, I have trouble relating well and feeling understood by people who have *perfect* relationships with their *perfect* kids.

I'd rather be a *real* parent with *real* children, even knowing authenticity can be painful, than risk further insult or injury to an already hurting parent. Parents who are in agony over the actions of their teenagers in rebellion don't need to be shown how the ideal parent would handle any given situation. Most parents want to be released from guilt, not locked into it.

Being real isn't easy. Sometimes it makes you cry. It means to open your heart for others to examine and to grow into a whole person—*believable.* I couldn't explain *real* better than a dialogue in a children's book, *The Velveteen Rabbit,* between an old skin horse and a new toy rabbit.

> "What is REAL?" asked the Rabbit.... "Does it mean having things that buzz inside you and a stick-out handle?"
>
> "Real isn't how you are made," said the Skin Horse. "It's a thing that happens to you. When a child loves you for a long, long time, not just to play with, but REALLY loves you, then you become Real."
>
> "Does it hurt?" asked the Rabbit.
>
> "Sometimes," said the Skin Horse, for he was always truthful. "When you are Real you don't mind being hurt."
>
> "Does it happen all at once, like being wound up," he asked, "or bit by bit?"
>
> "It doesn't happen all at once," said the Skin Horse. "You become. It takes a long time. That's why it doesn't happen to people who break easily, or have sharp edges, or have to be carefully kept. Generally, by the time you are Real, most of your hair has been loved off, and your eyes drop out and you get loose in the joints and very shabby. But all these things don't matter at all, because once you are Real you can't be ugly, except to people who don't understand."
>
> from *The Velveteen Rabbit*
> MARGERY WILLIAMS

THE DECLARATION OF A REAL PARENT

Being real has not resulted in hair loss or loose joints—a little loose skin maybe—but I'm still altogether. It has, however, worked off a few sharp edges and thinned my skin a bit. As I worked at being real, my facade of perfectionism finally faded. Through the experience of turning from "ideal," I developed guidelines which I named "The Declaration of a Real Parent." Perhaps they can help you stay in tune with reality.

- I am a parent to my children—not a peer.
- I am here to guide and direct my children, not to keep them constantly amused. I am a person, apart from the children, with needs and concerns of my own.
- I understand parenting is not a simple task. There are no magic formulas.
- I will be honest in my discussions with other parents, taking care not to pretend I am the *Mythical, Model Parent.*
- I will be *real,* with my children as well as with other parents in my prayer or support groups.
- I will help other parents in their struggle to be authentic, with a listening ear and with sympathetic understanding.

When we are real, we become transparent. We can care, forgive, love, and be loved in return. If you still have questions about being yourself, ask your family. If there's one thing I've learned through life with my teenagers, it's that no one knows the *real me* like my family!

SIX STEPS TO FINDING THE REAL YOU

1. Be willing to show your warts as well as your beauty marks.

2. Don't be afraid to share true feelings with the people you love and are close to.

3. Allow the free flow of tears and laughter. Don't stifle yourself.

4. Tell your children when you hurt—encourage them to do the same. Show them laughter when you're tickled. Cry in your pain. Shout in your anger. Love in all things.

5. Refuse to isolate yourself as an anomaly or an abnormal parent if your children aren't the people you've reared them to be. There are many parents, who, like me, need to know they are not alone.

6. If you really want to get radical, share your real self with strangers. You'll find the strangers quickly become friends when you trust them enough to share.

8

Learn to Be a Good Loser

With so few ideal parents and perfect kids in the world, most of us have waved good-bye to our Perfect Parent Award forever. Along with the crumbling facade of perfectionism, life with teenagers brings varying degrees of troubles, trials, and tribulation. This suffering facilitates the need for another strategy—that of learning the art of gracious suffering.

THE BITTER TASTE OF SUFFERING

I discovered this need in myself a little over two years ago. August had just overtaken July, and Caryl outdistanced thirteen by a month and a half. The reality of being an imperfect parent tormented me, as I watched the fireworks display of the setting summer sun. The splotches of reds, oranges, pinks, and lavenders, that would ordinarily dazzle me, faded hazily into the background, as I frantically searched the nearby streets for my teenage daughter.

Seven-thirty. It would be dark soon. I pulled the car into the driveway, and within minutes resumed my post at the living-room window. *It's all my fault,* I reminisced. *She's such a sensitive kid. If only I hadn't gotten sarcastic and irritated. I should have had more patience.*

I'd asked her to get the dishes done by noon. When I came home from shopping at three-thirty, they still hadn't been done. My patience thinned. "Caryl," I reminded, "these dishes aren't going to wash themselves."

"In a minute, Mom," answered the sweet, televisionized voice.

"Your minute's up. I asked you to do them five hours ago."

"Oh, Mom, this show's almost over. . . ."

"Young lady," I interrupted, "turn off that idiot box right now and get these dishes done!"

Sparks of hostility flew out of every muscle, as she stuffed the dishwasher and ran a rag over the counters. *Hmmm,* I thought, *maybe I shouldn't have raised my voice. But . . . what could I do? I thought I was being strong and honest—I even added a little joke. I guess she didn't see the humor. Well, I certainly was honest. I hate Saturday television.*

"Honey," I tried to soothe things over, "I'm sorry, but. . . ."

An icy glare interrupted me and declared war.

"I'm going out!" She grabbed an apple and bombed out the door and down the street on her bike.

Caryl never reacted like this. Sure, she'd go in her room and sulk for a day or two, but . . . it's been almost four hours. Guilt, grief, and anguish filled me. *Will she come home? Is she safe?*

Just as I headed out for the sixth time to search the neighborhood, I spotted her rounding the corner, heading for home.

"Where have you been?" I scolded as I held her tight. "I've been worried sick about you. Don't you *ever* take off like that again, without letting me know where you are."

"Mom," she patronized, "you shouldn't worry. I'm not a baby anymore. I just went for a bike ride and visited a couple of friends till I could cool off."

She just wanted to *cool off.* I had spent the last four hours *heating up.* It took me three days to undo the knots in my stomach.

As I thought about the pain I suffered in that ordeal, I wondered what I'd do in a real crisis. I mean, this was nothing compared to what some of my friends had gone through.

Take, for example, my friend Sandy and the trials she's had with her fifteen-year-old daughter, Jamie. Sandy had called me a few days before my run-in with Caryl.

"I need you to pray for us," Sandy's voice broke. She cried. After a few minutes she continued, "It's Jamie—she's pregnant."

"Oh, Sandy," I stammered, "I'm so sorry. What can I do to help?"

"Just pray for now. I know everything will work out somehow. It . . . it's not the pregnancy so much . . . worse than that . . . she wants an abortion."

Pregnant. Abortion. The words rang sickeningly in my ears. If anything like that happened to Caryl, I don't know if I could handle it. Up until the kids hit their teens, I hardly knew the meaning of suffering. Now, with two teenagers and the trials they can bring, I decided I'd better be prepared.

SUFFERING—A GIFT FROM GOD?

My first step in developing a strategy for gracious suffering was to contact my good friend Marge. Sometimes I imagined Marge as one of God's computers. I think of her brain as a large file in which she's stored an answer to every possible question or need anyone could have. Actually, Marge is very human. She's one of those older, wiser women who shares her experience and wisdom with still-learning people like me.

"Marge," I asked, "what good does all this suffering, pain, and sorrow do? Why does God allow it? And, I guess my biggest question right now is, how can I learn to cope with it?"

You can imagine my shock when my friend told me, "The best way to learn how to handle trials and suffering is to accept each one as a gift from God."

A gift from God? What a profound statement. It sort of goes along with the idea of "rejoice in all things," and, of course, that includes suffering. As I researched the problem, I found Marge was right.

The biblical basis for her statement appears in James 1:2, 3: "Count it all joy, my brethren, when you meet various trials, for you know that the testing of your faith produces steadfastness." Also, check out Romans 5:3: ". . . we rejoice in our sufferings, knowing that suffering produces endurance."

So you see, according to the Bible, we're all to rejoice over our troubles, trials, and tribulations. Personally, I'm convinced those words were written specifically for parents of teenagers. They certainly are appropriate for me. Ever since my oldest turned thirteen, I've been given one opportunity after another to learn the mysterious art of gracious suffering.

CLIMBING PAIN MOUNTAIN

These days, I consider myself a semigracious sufferer. (I'm still learning.) It's been a long and weary trip. Let me share with you some of the rough spots in my travels up Pain Mountain. Actually, these were talks I had with God along the way. I call them the *Lamentations of Pat.*

"Oh, Lord, [I cried one night after Dave captured the illusive driver's license] if suffering is so good for me, why does it hurt?

"If You love me—and I'm sure You do—how can You let me suffer like this? It's Saturday night. My son isn't home. He drives with the reckless abandon of a kamikaze pilot. As I pace the floor, worry gives me lessons in insomnia. Anxiety has my fingernails chewed to the nubs. I can't take much more.

"Lord, You are a God of love. You want me to be happy, don't You? You have the power to do everything and change *anything*. Why don't You take away my suffering? I'm not cut out to be a 'hurting parent.' What's wrong with a carefree life?

"Lord, my kids' 'growing pains' are killing me. At times the pain is so intense, I can't talk—only cry. A choking lump lodges in my throat. I can feel the hurt pushing deep into my chest . . . it's hard to breathe. The sharp pain pierces my stomach, and I rock to make it go away.

"Is this Your idea of a learning experience, Lord? How can I learn from pain? How can this make me a better parent? How can I be gracious when my eyes are red and my laugh lines turn to rivers for my tears?

"You know what You're doing—I think . . . I mean, I know. It's just . . . sometimes I don't understand why."

THE SECRET OF PEACEFUL SUFFERING

I suffered loud. I yelled at God, and moaned and groaned. Then, sometimes, I suffered in silence, isolated, numb, and depressed. As I struggled through, I came to understand suffering as an important, strengthening, and uplifting way of life. One day my wise friend, Marge, gave me a book called *Let Go*, by Fénelon. I didn't think I was hanging on, but I read it anyway. By the time I got to the second page, I knew this book was talking to me.

"How to Bear Suffering Peacefully" was the chapter title. I won't quote him, because, frankly, Fénelon comes off pretty heavy and theological. Since he wrote this stuff during the seventeenth century, it's no wonder. Using modern terms, he might say something like this: When useless thoughts occupy your head, throw them out. Concentrate instead on how you can love others. Then you can feel high, even when times are tough.

What are *useless thoughts?* As an example, the story I told about Caryl at the beginning of this chapter was full of them. Phrases such as, "It's my fault," or thoughts that begin with "What if . . ."; or "if only . . ." are useless.

I shouldn't have worried or blamed myself. Ideally, those four frantic hours during Caryl's absence would have been better spent in prayer, and in thinking helpful, positive thoughts. Hmmm . . . I wonder if I'll ever be able to stop worrying about my kids. I doubt it. It's a good thing gracious suffering doesn't demand perfection.

Another piece of helpful information I lifted from Archbishop Fénelon's book was that I should be willing to accept my burdens or sufferings without a fight. Suffering is easier when you develop a "spirit of nonresistance"!

Some of my friends tell me I hang on too long. Maybe they're right. It's hard not to resist pain, yet as a nurse, I certainly understand the concept of accepting the pain and rolling with the punches.

In my nursing duties at the clinic, I've often helped a patient through a painful procedure with words of reassurance. "Breathe deep. Easy. Don't fight it. Try to relax. I know it hurts, but work with it. The pain will end soon." A soothing voice and hand held in comfort helps the patient bear the pain. Somehow the pain becomes more bearable, not because of what is said or done, but because someone cares and understands. The patient has the reassurance that the pain will eventually give way to healing.

Work with it. Sometimes we need to suffer in order for life to improve. Me? I guess I need suffering and painful experiences to stay close to God. Often, when things go too well, I get spiritually lazy, and forget to pray and thank God. I forget to meditate and study God's Word. It usually takes some kind of minor crisis to bring me back to reality and back into the Bible. C. S. Lewis writes in his book *The Problem of Pain,* "God whispers to us in our pleasures, speaks in our conscience, but shouts in our pain."

For me, at least, pain and suffering seem to be God's way of getting my attention.

MY ROLE MODEL FOR SUFFERING

As I grew to be a gracious sufferer, I had a role model. My friend Joan had undergone more trials than the Supreme Court. Joan taught me that suffering can make a person stronger and better equipped to handle all areas of life. For all the problems she encountered in the rearing of her seven children, the boating accident which claimed the life of her husband and oldest son, and her own intense physical pain, there is no hint of bitterness and resentment.

In fact, she started a support group for hurting parents of teenagers in her church and worked vigorously in a hospice program for cancer patients.

"One of my kids died at eighteen. Another one couldn't cope with that death, blamed God, and turned to drugs. My seventeen-year-old daughter ran off with a forty-year-old married man, and they are living together. I guess you could say I know what it means to suffer. I just want people to know there is hope." Joan died of lung cancer. She left me with her philosophy of suffering.

"God allows us all a time to suffer," Joan shared during the final days of her illness. "He expects us to walk into it, grow through it, and walk out of it. While we're in it, we can mourn, cry, and anguish. Then, the growth in suffering is the newfound empathy with which you can comfort and help others."

Joan's exemplary way of suffering reminded me of something I'd read in William Barclay's commentary on *The Gospel of Luke,* in which he writes about the prophetess, Anna, and the effect of sorrow (Luke 2:36–40).

Anna was a widow. She had known sorrow and she had not grown bitter. Sorrow can do one of two things to us. It can make us kinder, softer, more sympathetic. It can despoil us our faith; or it can root faith even deeper. It all depends on how we think of God. If we think of Him as a tyrant we will resent Him. If we think of Him as Father we too will be sure that

> A Father's hand will never cause
> His child a needless tear.

THE QUALITIES OF A GRACIOUS SUFFERER

Joan glowed with the joy of knowing and trusting God through her trials. Her smile and her love-brightened face lightened the path of many, and directed them to God. Joan taught me what it means to be a gracious sufferer. She knew what it meant to take a punch and bounce back.

With the help of several other parents who have learned how to take a punch, I developed a checklist to remind myself of the qualities of a gracious sufferer.

As a gracious sufferer, I have the ability to:

_____ accept both my teenagers and troubles as a gift from God.

_____ accept each trial and tribulation without resistance.

_____ walk into my time of suffering and cry. Walk out again— fortified with God's love.

_____ trust in the promises of God's Word, and know He has a handle on the situation, no matter how gloomy things may seem.

_____ reject guilt and know that suffering, in the right proportions, is therapeutic.

_____ relax and let God teach me the lesson I'm supposed to learn.

_____ love the one who hurt me. Grow in Christ without bitterness or resentment.

_____ keep my heart and mind focused on Jesus. In every pain, I

visualize how He suffered for me, then I can go on to bear
my burdens—graciously.
____ reach out to help others.

How did you do? Don't be discouraged if you weren't able to
check them all. When I first started my self-improvement program in gracious suffering, I could only check one or two. My
positive attitude kept me pushing for more. Now, I'm close to
100 percent but I still have trouble with resentment and nonresistance. So keep trying; it will come.

WE'RE ALL IN THE SAME DINGHY

There is yet another facet of suffering. To suffer opens the
door to being real, or being honest and open with other parents. Many times parents have come up to me after a discussion on the painful problems of raising teenagers and thanked
me for sharing. "I've had those same problems with my kids.
It's good to know I'm not alone."

As far as I'm concerned, no parent of teenagers is alone;
we're almost all in the same dinghy. I say *almost* because there
are a few parents who are still standing serenely on the shore.

While all of us will encounter various trials and sufferings at
some time in our lives, not every parent will have troubles with
their children. If you are one of the fortunate few who aren't
treading water with your teenagers, give the rest of us
strugglers a break. Try not to be smug if your kids are well be-
haved. I know it's difficult to empathize without the trial of
personal experience, but try. If my own children weren't providing me with firsthand experience, I might not be quite as
understanding of the parent in pain.

Most of us have felt pain and suffered in one form or another. Believe me, the pain parents feel when one of their own
is messed up can be agonizing. Remember to treat other parents with kindness, be gentle and understanding with one an-

other. You never know when you might end up in the same boat.

Meanwhile back in the dinghy—if you find yourself in rough water, there's little to do but don your lifejacket and ride it out.

I had a friend tell me that if I praised and thanked God for everything—even suffering—I'd be floating on the Sea of Tranquility. Well, I'm a Christian, and I say a lot of *thank Yous* to God, but I'm still sailing in my salt-water dinghy, and sometimes the waves are enormous. Life *doesn't* simply and miraculously settle into easy living. Consequently, most of us could use a few lessons in how to relax and ride out the storm.

FIRST-AID KIT FOR GRACIOUS SUFFERERS

To keep you from falling out of your dinghy and better cope with suffering, you will want to stock up on a few items for your soul-patching first-aid kit.

You will need to be well supplied with biblical principles and promises. These will ease you through sleepless nights and agonizing defeats. Keep a Bible available at all times to remind you of God's promises. Mark your Bible well. Underscore the passages which will best help you remember that God is with you. Along with the verses I've already mentioned, these have been especially helpful to me.

Now to him who by the power at work within us is able to do far more abundantly than all that we ask or think.
Ephesians 3:20

Rest in the Lord; wait patiently for him to act....
Psalms 37:7 TLB

I will not leave you comfortless: I will come to you.
John 14:18 KJV

They that sow in tears shall reap in joy.

Psalms 126:5 KJV

Along with collecting promises, you will need to maintain a groundwork of faith. Pray daily for the faith and strength you need to get you through the rough seas ahead. Trust God to bring you and your children safely through to Him.

Despite strong faith and the Bible at your side, tears, failure, and inadequacy will attack. You may even find yourself imprisoned by depression.

During these unfortunate moments, hours, or days of suffering, Satan will probably try to convince you that worry is a way of life, and if you don't at least *worry* about your children, your attitude or parental ability would be worthless. Your fears may show you an image of the worst possible outcome of your child's misdeeds. Oh, and let's not forget guilt. Guilt will most likely convince you the whole mess is your fault. Your home-brewed guilt and Satan may even have you thinking, "A Christian shouldn't be crying, worrying, or getting ulcers. You're afraid God won't come through and make things right. You should be ashamed. What kind of Christian are you?"

If I painted a bleak picture, forgive me. But, suffering does have a way of opening the door to guilt and worry—and Satan. An important point to remember is that whether your teenager mouths off, steals from you, runs away from home, or whatever, you have every reason to feel hurt. And, second, blaming yourself will only compound the problem. Don't be ashamed or feel guilty over tears, discouragement, or even anger. God gave each of us the gift of tears and the ability to express various emotions. Perhaps it would be helpful for you to think of sorrow in this way: the tears of our sorrows become the rainbow of tomorrow. Without rain, we'd have no rainbow.

Life with teenagers can bring storms of grief, but it can also bring gales of laughter, a whirlwind of joy, and a flood of sunshine. Be careful not to let guilt, Satan, and sorrow hide the sun.

Last Saturday, my angry teenage son sent up storm warnings. I donned my lifejacket (love) and secured myself to the mainmast (God). Dave blew with the fury of a hurricane. I waited for the sun. It came.

A PARENT'S GUIDE TO GRACIOUS SUFFERING

1. Develop the "spirit of nonresistance." Be real and go with the flow. In other words, let it happen. Nonresistive suffering can produce fruits of: new insight, compassion, empathy, deeper love and concern for others; commitment to God, and acceptance of God's will.

2. Understand that God knows what He's doing and won't allow you to suffer beyond your ability to endure it. God will provide the necessary strength (1 Corinthians 10:13).

3. Remember, any suffering turned inward or held too long may lead to despair, chronic depression, bitterness, and resentment. It then becomes useless and self-destructive.

4. There are various natural steps in the grieving process. As you suffer through various trials, expect to experience some or all of these emotions: shock; uncontrolled tears; brief periods of anger (toward God, self, or others); denial, which moves toward acceptance; and periodic depression.

Submit to these emotions. Let them come and go. This will allow you to work through the grieving process naturally. Suppression or resistance may produce prolonged negative effects. Simmered anger eventually reaches a boiling point.

5. As you learn to allow yourself the gift of suffering, learn also to allow others to suffer. Here are some thoughts to remember when comforting a hurting friend.

    a. Helpful hints aren't helpful when you hurt.

    b. Avoid inhibiting remarks like, "Don't cry"; or "Don't

think about it." In fact, it's best to avoid *don't* altogether.

c. A broken heart doesn't need to be reminded, "It will all work out for the best."

d. Be natural. Say what you feel, such as, "I'm sorry," or "I can't believe it," or "I wish I could help."

e. If you can't say anything, that's okay too. Just sit quietly, cry, and pray.

f. A squeeze of the hand, a touch, or a hug indicate love and concern without the need for words.

> When sorrow came
>> with tears and pain,
>> a friend embraced me.
> "I'm so sorry . . ." were her only words.
>> Then—we cried.
> A burden lightened for me that day,
>> My friend carried half of it away.

9

Love Your Teenager as Yourself

It was Agatha Christie who said, "If you love, you will suffer, and if you do not love, you do not know the meaning of a Christian life." Love is linked tightly with suffering. In fact, love is woven into each of the other five strategies. It becomes the foundation on which a positive attitude, joy, strength, authenticity, and gracious suffering are built. Without love these strategies are nothing.

My conclusion is based on the matchless words of the apostle Paul in 1 Corinthians 13:1–3. As I thought about these words and their meaning for parents of teenagers, a paraphrase came to me:

> If I speak positively at all times and find joy in all things, but lack unlimited love, my efforts are for nothing. And, if I have the strength to overcome my guilt and my weaknesses, and gain openness and understanding of all the mysteries surrounding teenage behavior, but lack love, I am empty. If I learn to suffer for my children's sake, but can't love them enough to forgive and forget, I am useless. If I give them everything I possess and all my time, but cannot give them unconditional love, I lose it all.

HOW SECURE IS MY LOVE FOUNDATION?

When I thought about how much of the relationship with my teenagers is based on love, and how important love is to the whole family structure, I decided I'd better inspect and evaluate my foundation. Is my love strong enough to build on?

I used to think so. No other mother or father loved their children any more than I did. But, as they scrambled into their teens, I developed doubts and conflicting ideas about love. Of course, along with the doubts came the guilt.

I could get thrown out of the Good Parents League for this, but there are times when I actually wonder, *Do I really love my kids?*

The other day is an example. Loud, disgruntled sounds ricocheted up the stairs from the family room.

"Mom!" Caryl screamed, "David's hitting me."

"I am not! I just barely touched her. She's trying to get me in trouble again, as usual."

"Aarrgh," Caryl muttered, tight-lipped and tight-fisted, as she stomped up the stairs, through the kitchen, and down the hall to her room. "Can't you do something about *him!* I hate him!" Her bedroom door slammed shut, and the aftershock rattled the windows.

"Hey, Mom! This whole thing is yours and Dad's fault, you know," Dave reminded. "You could have been happy with me, an only child; but no, you had to have a girl."

Guilt covered me like a blanket, as I thought, *Yeah, and I might have been even happier with none.* I winced at the thought. I'm a mother. How can a mother think like that? Like it or not, too many times, I find myself faced with teenagers who frequently push me beyond my endurance and ability to love and cope with their unloving attitudes.

I logically concluded that I would need more than a superficial kind of love to survive my teenagers. This job calls for "superlove"—an unlimited, unconditional love, like ... like God's love.

LOVE—BY GOD'S STANDARDS

Since there is no more perfect, loving parent than God, I reviewed what His Book had to say on the subject. I found the best description of God's love in 1 Corinthians 13:

> Love is patient and kind; love is not jealous or boastful; it is not arrogant or rude. Love does not insist on its own way; it is not irritable or resentful; it does not rejoice at wrong, but rejoices in the right. Love bears all things, believes all things, hopes all things, endures all things.... So faith, hope, love abide, these three; but the greatest of these is love.

I don't know about you, but as I read those verses, I saw even more shortcomings in myself. There are many times, at least in my family, when the feelings we show for each other are far removed from the *love* God intended. We try to be loving. Unfortunately, we too often create an unloving mess, which seems contrary to anything I ever learned about God's love.

For instance, when my kids get sassy, I'd like to punch 'em out. Then I wonder if God ever wants to wallop *me*. No doubt, I've caused Him a fair amount of grief. Surprisingly, though, from all I understand about God, He continues to forgive and love me in the most perfect way; which, by the way, is miraculous when I think about how short-tempered I can be.

To illustrate, let me tell you about a problem I had last month. I'd had it with my family's demands.

"Mom, I need my gym clothes."

"Mom, didn't you wash my underwear?"

"Mom, why don't you ever bake bread? Kelly's mom bakes every day."

"Mom, I need to eat dinner by 4:30." [It was 4:15.]

"Honey, have you seen my car keys?"

"What are you guys? Helpless? Do I have to do everything around here?" I was not kind. I locked myself in the bathroom. *A bath will make me feel better,* I assured myself.

Just about the time I settled back into my luxurious bubble bath, someone pounded frantically on the bathroom door.

"Hurry up, Mom! I need to use the bathroom."

"I need the curling iron. I gotta leave in twenty minutes."

"When are we gonna eat dinner?"

"Can't you guys take a hint? I want to be alone!" My anger simmered near the boiling point. Guilt manifested itself, as I thought about God's love: "love is not irritable or resentful." I leveled accusations at myself. *You're being selfish! You don't care about anyone but yourself.*

How could I enjoy a bubble bath while drowning in guilt? I gave up. "I'm sorry," I finally admitted to my family. "I shouldn't get so irritated, but honestly, sometimes you drive me bananas."

Boy, I said to myself, *with me on the giving end instead of God, love sure loses its glory. I think it's time for another talk with God:*

Lord, this unconditional love I should have for my children overwhelms and confuses me. Your version of love has me baffled. Because You are God, You love Your children perfectly. But, what about me? I can't fill Your shoes. As the perfect loving parent, I'm a flop.

How about helping me straighten out my misconceptions in loving my teenagers and show me how to build a secure, unfailing foundation of love. Thanks, Lord.

Even after talking to God, I still felt crummy about the kind of love I give (or don't give) my kids. Is it possible—could I *ever* come to the point of unlimited, unconditional love?

LOVE YOUR TEENAGE "ENEMIES"

Nearly everyone knows the Bible tells us to "Love your neighbor as yourself." It also says, "Love your enemies." Sometimes I'm not sure which category my teenagers fit into. But, regardless of the category, I *do* love my kids.

Unfortunately, my love for them undergoes stresses and strains as our children progress (regress?) into adolescence. At that magical time, many teenagers feel peer-pressurized into taking on the role of "enemy." Some become unloving and insist they no longer need their parents' love.

I'm reminded of an interesting encounter I had with Dave not long ago. I discovered, much to my joy, that Dave and I both possessed a little more godly love toward each other than I'd previously thought.

"DAVE, DO YOU LOVE ME?"

I'm a potter. Usually, I don't let broken pots, warps, and stress cracks bother me. A break means "Oops, try again." Lately, however, my body stiffens whenever Dave walks into my studio. I mean, usually, doing pottery settles me down, and I can cope with anything.

This alteration in my calmness is understandable. Over the

last few months, accidents have followed Dave around like a security blanket. A few weeks ago, for example, we went out for pizza. He insisted he could handle the pizza server's role. When our number came up, dexterous Dave carried our pizza waiter-style—one hand, tray over head.

As he made the swooping delivery, he forgot to account for gravity and tilt. The pizza gracefully slipped from its tray and colored his Dad with red sauce, orange cheese, and green peppers. A spicy father/son encounter ensued.

What's this got to do with my pottery? Unfortunately, his accidents didn't stop with the pizza. Not long after the great pizza bash, he accidentally broke one of my favorite, hand-thrown, miniature vases, dropped a board on a freshly thrown casserole dish, and ruined several paint brushes because he forgot to clean them.

The other day as I worked at my potter's wheel, Dave moved through my studio with the grace of Paul Bunyan at a tea party. "Dave, please be careful," I moaned, eyeing my tray of wet cups.

"Don't worry," he assured. "I won't wreck any of your precious pots." He teasingly swung his hand, pretending to slay a few cups.

I reacted unlovingly. "Get your dangerous body out of here. One step closer and I'll turn you in for vandalism." I half-smiled to let him know I was only partly serious. "I've put a lot of work into this stuff."

"I'm sure. Are those pots more important than me?"

"Give me a minute. I'll have to think about it," I muttered.

Hmmm ... maybe he's right. Another guilt seed took root in my muddled mind. Do I love my pottery more than my kids?

My pots don't talk back to me. I can mold them and color them any way I want. They never complain; nor are they disrespectful. True, they couldn't love me back, but then my son isn't doing a hot job of that right now either.

"Dave," I asked seriously, "do *you* love me?"

"No!"

Hmmm . . . my first impulse was to feel sorry for myself, but I gave him another chance. "Do you love me?"

"That's a dumb question."

Well, that's better. I'll try again. "Dave, do you love me?"

With an embarrassed grin, he turned and mumbled, "Weird."

Although I didn't get quite the reply I had hoped for from David, I did get a few answers from God. I realized that Dave and a lot of other kids feel uncomfortable and often don't know how to express love to parents. I know Dave is filled with the need to "break away." So, to tell me, "I love you," why . . . it would be embarrassing and an outright admission of dependency.

I could have taken Dave's failure to express love to me as rejection and ended up feeling hurt and guilty. I know some parents who do just that. Recently, a father I know asked, "What's the use? Why should I put out all this effort to love someone who doesn't love me in return?" I can understand how this man felt. His son had completely turned away from his family and was heavily into drugs.

No, I thought to myself, *I can't fall into that kind of hopelessness. My kids might be ornery, impolite, angry, or rebellious, but wherever they are, I love Dave and Caryl more than my pottery. No contest. Decision confirmed.* I grabbed the pot I was forming on the wheel and squooshed it between my fingers and tossed it in the scrap bucket.

While this symbolic maneuver may not seem like much, it opened a whole new outlook for me on parental love. While my love is not perfect, I am capable, at least in a small degree, of unlimited, unconditional love. With God's help, I could even love my kids as enemies. Now I feel good about the way I love them, without feeling guilty over my imperfections.

If you're still feeling rejected and torn over your teenager's lack of love, and you think the love you've poured into your children seems to have vanished completely, maybe this poem will help. I wrote it to remind me that this "hidden-love syndrome" won't last forever.

WHERE IS THE LOVE?

What happened? Where is the love?
You know ... the love I planted in my child
    everyday, for seventeen years—and more.
It filtered in and sank.
Buried now beneath the ruins of bold, assertive,
    independent brass.
My love was constant, sure.
I planted plenty, and deep.
Someday the seeds will grow.
Love will blossom and overflow,
    someday—when the child becomes. . . .

Becomes? When Dave becomes a man, Caryl a woman ... when love turns from inside to outside ... when they find a special someone to share a home and family with ... then, the love I planted will produce a bumper crop. It will multiply itself a hundred times a hundred. I'm positive.

THE UNBROKEN CIRCLE OF LOVE

Whew! It feels good to be on a positive track again. You see, the big mistake I made was in placing too much emphasis on how I felt about my children and how they felt about me. When this single relationship crumpled or threatened extinction, I panicked. I forgot to take into account the whole circle of love which makes up our family unit. This continuous, unbroken circle keeps love going, even if a couple of the components turn up missing for a while. Consequently, if one or both of my kids turn prodigal, God, Ron and I, and maybe some special friends and relatives maintain a holding pattern until they return.

I suppose the easiest way to explain the strategy for this unbroken circle of unconditional, unlimited love, is to use my family as an example. God, Ron and I, and David and Caryl, as the primary family unit, form a circle. With a symbolic gesture, we hold hands, to create an unbroken circle of love. (Keep in mind, the actual circle is made with our hearts and minds.)

Let's suppose, David were to break his hold. He might angrily shout, "I hate you!" and leave home. Dave's absence would create a temporary gap. The rest of the family would take immediate action to expand our love by joining our hearts and minds together to close the circle.

Once again, the circle is whole and unbroken. "But, what about Dave," you may be asking. "Did you shut him out?"

On the contrary. As we reformed our circle, we drew Dave inside. This action constitutes a very important principle.

Physically, Dave could break away from our circle, but emotionally and mentally, he remains securely bonded to us in love. He may reject us, but our love refuses to reject him, or leave him out.

Hopefully, the one who breaks formation will come back to claim his or her place and work to maintain the circle of love. Children may break in and out of the circle many times during their teenage years. Sadly, some may never come back.

Dad may slip off for Bermuda on a business trip and never return. Mom may take up residence in Fiji without the family. One of the family members may die. But, as long as there are two, God and you, the circle can never be broken. From that strategic point, the circle originates.

GOD IS STILL NUMBER ONE

As I see it, there are four major components in this circle of love. It begins with our personal relationship with God, spreads out to include love for ourselves, and our spouse, then our teenagers (when available) complete the circle.

In our circle's origin (love from and for God), we develop the ability to love all others. "We love, because God first loved us." Without His love, we would be as ineffective in pouring out love as an empty pitcher.

For example, have you ever felt all loved out? Have you been confronted with a time when you felt that you had nothing left to give? I have.

It happened several years ago. As a new pediatric nurse, I wanted to give special attention to all my young patients, especially those who were dying. I would rock them and hold them. I comforted them and poured my love into them. As each one died, I felt drained. One night as I held a tiny, lifeless infant in my arms for the last time, the emptiness overwhelmed me. "I can't do this anymore," I cried. "I want to love, but there's no more love in me."

My good friend Marilyn, also a nurse, wisely counseled me. "Pat, you can't keep giving love if you shut off the source. Everybody needs to be replenished. God does that. Slow down. Let God love you. When He fills you up, you'll have more than enough love to carry you through."

LOVE YOURSELF

The second portion of the circle of love is filled with love for yourself. Remember, the Bible says, "Love your neighbor [teenager] *as* yourself. . . ." It doesn't say *more than,* but *as.* I don't mean to send you on an all-out ego trip. I simply ask that you be aware of a basic principle.

God loves you, He made you—He sent His Son to die for you, right? You are important. So, be patient and kind to yourself; care about yourself. In doing so, you will be better able to care for and love others. Relax in the luxury of solitude, meditation, and time off. In other words, let God love you. Realize, that in those times, God is revitalizing you so you can more effectively love your teenagers.

When you come up angry, defensive, or grouchy, realize

God still loves and forgives you, and you can then forgive yourself. This loving and forgiving attitude toward yourself also works to extinguish guilt.

LOVE YOUR SPOUSE

The third component of our circle of love is the relationship between husband and wife. It is placed in this order of priority, because, when the children are gone to form their own circle, the husband-wife relationship is the only one left in the home.

To illustrate my point, let me tell you about a discussion a friend of mine had with her teenage daughter a few days ago.

Fifteen-year-old Kelly fumed when her father insisted she change out of her bathrobe and do some housework.

"Who does *he* think he is? I can wear anything I want. This is *my* house, *my* body and *my* business," Kelly shouted at her mother. "He's always causing trouble. Why don't you just divorce him. We don't need him."

"It seems to me, you've lost track of who's boss around here," Marie replied. "You've apparently forgotten your place. May I remind you, your father's and my relationship comes first. We started this family and we're going to finish it—together. When you grow up and start your own family, you'll establish the rules. In this family, your dad and I make the rules."

"You don't love me, do you?"

"Kelly, your dad and I love you and will always love you. But, first we love each other."

The thoughtful expression on Kelly's face told Marie, maybe—just maybe—she'd gotten through.

CIRCLE YOUR TEENAGER WITH LOVE

The fourth area of our unbroken circle includes the love we have for our children. This is often the most transient portion of the circle. By drawing on the other three, we can keep the circle unbroken. Because God loves me, I can love God, myself, my husband, and my teenagers—even when they think they don't love me.

Teenagers need to know their parents love them—no matter what. Keeping this circle of love intact requires words as well as actions on your part. My plan for fulfilling this purpose goes like this:

I keep my mind focused on a parent's version of "Love is. . . ."

- Love is a gift from God.
- Love is caring about myself enough to accept my mistakes, to try again, and keep loving.
- Love is the ability to say and mean, "I love you"—unconditionally.

If you don't already express love to your kids, start now. At least once a day, pull out a hug and an "I love you." If you haven't said it for a while, because one of your offspring thinks "it's dumb," say it anyway. Practice.

If your son breaks curfew and gets arrested, say, "I love you." If your daughter gets busted for possession of drugs, say, "I love you." Whatever the disaster, hug your teenager, and say, *"I love you!"*

An unbroken circle of love forms a foundation that can be built on. Not even guilt or Satan can undermine it.

The formation of this unbroken circle completes the six strategies needed to plunge fearless and guiltless into life with teenagers.

SIX WAYS TO SECURE YOUR FOUNDATION OF LOVE

1. Love requires an open vessel in order to be received and given. Here is an exercise to show you how this concept works

Close your eyes. Envision yourself as a hollow tube. Decorate it any way you like. (Mine wears jeans and a smock.) See God continuously and unconditionally pouring love in. As the love filters through, it mixes with a unique and special *you*. Watch love bubble over in abundance, as you allow it to flow unceasingly through the opening at the other end. God created you, a vessel of love.

2. You deserve a hug today. Here is another exercise to make sure you get it.

Again, close your eyes. Stand with both feet firmly planted about a foot-and-a-half apart. Stretch both arms straight out in front of you. Spread your fingers wide apart. Bend your right elbow and place your right hand just behind and to the right of your left shoulder. Just so, bend your left elbow and place your left hand just behind and to the left of your right shoulder. Now, squeeze firmly. Say out loud, "Thanks, I needed that."

3. Hug yourself and your husband everyday—and your teenagers when you can find them.

4. Even if your teenagers wear the name ENEMY, love them. In your heart they will change from enemy to friend.

> He drew a circle that shut me out—
> Heretic, rebel, a thing to flout.
> But Love and I had the wit to win:
> We drew a circle that took him in.
>
> EDWIN MARKHAM
> *Outwitted*

5. When you feel all loved out, take time for refilling. Relax and let God love you. Lavish yourself in a day of solitude.

6. True unconditional love cannot be attained except through prayer, complete acceptance and expectation of *God's* love.
- Love through grace—not acquired but given.
- Open yourself—accept God.

PART III

HUGGING YOUR TEENAGER THROUGH IT ALL

In the last nine chapters, we uncovered the guilt scam and worked out six essential strategies for coping with guilt, while lovingly raising our teenagers.

In these last five chapters, you'll learn about a few major challenges in parenting, or "deparenting" teenagers. At the same time, you'll see where, when, and how the six strategies come into play.

Can you imagine life without humor or a positive attitude during your teenagers' bid for independence? How could a parent survive the communication gap without love, laughter, and authenticity? And, what would the food problems and the driving mania be like without inner strength, and the ability to suffer graciously. Of course, if and when the real problems hit, you'll need them all—but mostly, you'll need that unbroken circle of unlimited, unconditional love.

10

Gradual Deparenting *Versus* All-Out Independence

Independence! "Give me liberty—or I'll make life miserable for you," becomes the slogan of many adolescents who think they have matured.

This big push for freedom is an area of major conflict between parents and their teenagers. When the kids say, "I'm ready!" and the parents say, "You're not!" the communication gap widens. Both parents and teenagers are left frustrated, confused, and insecure. Both feel neither understands the other.

While our teenagers might be a little hesitant about "movin' on," the glamour of independent living compels them forward. Dreams of a car, an apartment, no rules, no lectures, no chores. . . . "Man, it'll be so-o-o cool."

While the kids go for *cool,* we parents often find ourselves *overheated,* as we struggle through the storms and try to get our kids out into society in one piece. There is no better place to use the six strategies from Part II than right here in Freedom Valley, where teenagers make their bid for independence.

A positive attitude and a sense of humor is a must as youngsters grow up and out. You can bet on having to be open and real during those "push-pull" episodes, and you'll probably have plenty of opportunities to turn weakness into strength. Of course, there will undoubtedly be time to practice graceful suffering, and always . . . always a chance to love your teenagers through it all.

Most moms and dads aren't too keen on the teenager's grasp for independence when it comes too quickly. They'd rather release their hold more gradually. Like me. I'd like to hand over more responsibility, but . . . are they ready? If I were to rate my kids' self-sufficiency IQ, some days, I'd score them nine on a scale of one to ten. Other days I'd rank them about minus one.

"BUT THAT'S WHAT MOMS ARE FOR"

My teenagers are no dummies. They've been responsible for getting themselves up in the morning since they were seven years old. They can cook, clean house, wash and dry their own clothes. Caryl even made a spoon out of seaweed once in Outdoor School.

Recently, she survived a three-day wilderness hike with her biology teacher and two other girls. Through rain-soaked tents and sleeping bags, hail, snow, blistered feet, and a chipmunk that died from eating their *yukky* macaroni and cheese, these pioneer women conquered the wilderness.

Quite a feat for a girl who just asked me, "Mom, when are you gonna mend my socks?"

"I think it's time you learned to mend your own clothes, honey. I'll be glad to teach you this afternoon," I graciously replied.

"Me? You want *me* to do it?" Then she added sweetly, "But, that's what moms are for."

How can I look at my children as ready to go it alone, when I'm still showered with outbursts such as, "Mom, where's my shoe?"

"Mom, didn't you wash my gym clothes?"

"Mom, why didn't you wake me up?"

"Mom! Where's breakfast? I'll have two eggs-over-easy, hashbrowns, toast, and Sizzlean, and don't forget the strawberry jam. Oh, yeah, and make me some coffee . . . okay?"

Out on their own? *My* kids? They can't even remember to take out the garbage. The other day I set the garbage bag in front of the door before they left for school. I even reminded them to take it. They left. Garbage stayed. That afternoon, one said, "I forgot." The other remarked, "I didn't see it."

And, that's not all. One day I noticed the toilet-paper holder needed a new roll. Someone had set a new roll of TP on the bathroom counter. *No,* I said to myself, *I won't do it. I'll wait and see how long it takes for one of my "independent" and responsible kids to notice the job needs doing.* Over the next few days I hinted. I gave them each step-by-step instructions on how to refill the holder. Finally, after two weeks and three rolls, I did it myself. "They need me," I decided, and suffered silently.

All this and they think they are ready to take on *more* responsibility? Or, maybe . . . maybe they're subtly hinting that they're not ready to leave. Maybe they're just trying to soften the blow for when they really do leave home.

Yes, that must be the case, because somehow, even with a positive attitude, I have trouble picturing my teenagers in a home of their own.

Dave's would be clean enough, I guess. It's his handling of money. . . . After he buys his car, stereo equipment, and steaks, will there be anything left for rent, electricity, water and all the other nonluxury items?

While Caryl tends to be a little more frugal, she may run into other problems. I can see her wading knee-deep in clothes, dust, dishes, and lists she made to get herself better organized. But she'd survive. After all, she knows how to make a spoon out of seaweed.

DEPARENTING IS A FINE ART

Anyway, you can see why I'm a little reluctant to cut all the apron strings completely. Thus, I'm caught in the middle of the age-old struggle of "Gradual Deparenting *Versus* All-Out Independence."

Before going any further, let me explain *deparenting*. Contrary to popular belief on the part of teenagers, *deparent* does not mean cancelation of parents or parental authority. My definition is this:

Deparent—a gradual transition from parent-controller to parent counselor. When your children are born, you are in complete control. But, as they grow older, your control lessens as you learn to "deparent" your child. In fact, deparenting begins almost as soon as the child is born.

Now that you're familiar with terms, let's get back to the problem. Unfortunately, gradual freedom (or gradual anything, for that matter) is an unbearable program for many headstrong teenagers.

When you stop and think about it, you can hardly blame the kids. After all, in a world of instant breakfasts, instant oatmeal, instant potatoes, and instant Jello, why can't there be instant adults?

TEENAGERS ARE A MODERN INVENTION

About 150 years ago, children did have to become instant adults. Teenagers, as we know them, were practically nonexistent. At twelve to fourteen, children were out working to help support their families. Opportunity for rebellion presented itself mostly among the wealthy, or those who found working for a living a bore. Quite simply, rebellious teenagers were not in vogue.

There was little time to dwell on theories of "Who am I?" or "It's my life; I'll live it my way."

Parents booted their kids out the door to independence before the ink had time to dry on the birth certificate. By the time they were my youngsters' ages, they were most likely married and supporting families of their own.

Today, many mothers fight like she-bears to hold on to their cubs until they are at least eighteen and "of age." Of course, we encourage them to finish high school and college. And, we add, "Please, don't get married till you're at least twenty."

Maybe over a hundred years ago, youngsters needed to get out and join the ranks of adults early in life. How many and whether or not they were ready to leave home, I can't say. I do know, however, with today's turbulent society and laws that force teens to remain dependent on parents until they're at least eighteen, I'll try to keep mine home and give them my support, until I think they're ready to leave.

My instincts and reality tell me my kids still need guidance and direction. In the Rushford family, we plan to influence our children as long as we can, and advise them as long as they'll listen. After all, fifty to one hundred years ago, parents didn't have to contend with compromises like television, *PG, R* and *X*-rated movies, porno books and magazines, and widespread use of drugs and alcohol.

MOTHER EAGLE'S APPROACH

My philosophy for growing youngsters up and out (or deparenting) is akin to the eagle's. When the eaglets are of age, Mother Eagle drops them one at a time from their nest, which is perched high on a cliff. As the eaglet falls, she encourages flight. When the babe loses strength and plummets, Mother swoops down, catches the eaglet on her back and returns it safely to the nest. With each release, the young eagle flies longer and farther, until, finally, Mother no longer needs to rescue and usher it securely home. The eagle achieves its independence.

Too many times human youngsters leap out of the nest while Mom's or Dad's back is turned. Then guess who's left to pick up the pieces and mend the broken wings?

Not every family is endowed with a nest jumper. Each child is different. Not only in the way they achieve their independence, but in the way they look at life. They also differ in the age at which they start ringing the bell of freedom.

"I DON'T WANNA' BE HUGGED!"

David's bid for independence began at age nine. Everytime I hugged him, his body stiffened like a Buckingham Palace Guard.

He refused to display any form of affection. "I don't wanna' be hugged," he grumbled.

At first he coolly accepted my motherly gestures; but by the fifth grade, not only did rigor mortis set in, he pushed me away and insisted, "I'm too old for all that mushy stuff."

In trying to console myself, I'd tell my friends, "It's just a phase he's going through."

I didn't give up. I kept hugging; he kept pushing. Finally, one day during his twelfth year of existence, the cold war ceased. We plunged head-on into hand-to-hand combat.

I reached out to hug him. He ducked, "No way, Mom! Cut it out!"

With my love strategy in mind, I refused to be rejected. I came at him again with the agility of a fencing master. He tried to elude my lunge, but he wasn't fast enough. I spun around, caught the back of his jeans and tackled him. The move propelled us both in a heap onto the rust-brown carpet. "You're not getting away," I panted. With herculean strength, I grabbed his arm and pinned him. After tickling him into submission, I collected my hug, pecked his cheek and fell back on the rug, exhausted.

You think I'm crazy, don't you? Going through all that trouble for a hug. You may be right, but whenever I see the old bumper sticker HAVE YOU HUGGED YOUR KID TODAY? I can say without an ounce of guilt, "Sure have!" Besides, it was worth the struggle—now sometimes he hugs me back.

"IT'S MY LIFE, I'LL DO WHAT I WANT!"

In Dave's strike for independence, rejection of my hugs constituted only the beginning. If this exclusion of motherly love had been the only problem, I could have handled parenting without the Maalox. But, stiffening up in my arms soon progressed to bellowing war cries that all sounded essentially the same: "It's my life; I'll do what I want!"

What I actually needed at this early stage in Dave's teenage career (and even before) were those six strategies laid out in chapters 4 through 9. While love had a good start, they all needed developing. We found ourselves unprepared for the next major episode of Dave's life, but it did provide an opportunity to learn and grow.

My friends tried to warn me. Unfortunately, I wasn't acting real. "No," I smugly remarked, "Dave would *never....*"

But he did. He ran away from home. I had come home from a meeting one night about nine-thirty and discovered Dave missing. He'd taken a sleeping bag and backpack, but left no clue as to where he'd gone or who he was with. As I paced the floor, I wondered *why?*

Dave was only fourteen, but worldly wise. According to his standards, Albert Einstein was "dumb." I couldn't believe this intelligent kid would actually leave home. I cried! I agonized! Despite Matthew 6:25, where Christ says, "Be not anxious . . ." I *was* anxious. The dull ache of worry throbbed through my body like an abscessed tooth.

Dave was gone. Ron and I no longer controlled our son or his actions. *Trust God,* echoed through my numb and confused brain. *Okay, Lord, he's Your kid too; You'll have to take over.*

Even after handing Dave over to God for safekeeping, I didn't feel much better—stronger, yes—but not better; at least not right away. I tried to maintain a positive attitude; but this runaway caper happened before I started my "Good Stuff" journal, so all my thinking came out in minuses. Then I tried to find some humor in the situation, but it was almost as funny as hemorrhoids. I did succeed in utilizing a couple of my strategies that night, though. Suffering excelled. I gave myself freedom to cry—didn't stifle myself at all. And *real* . . . I felt very, very real.

The next morning Ron and I found him—safe and exhausted. I wouldn't let him fall asleep until he'd relayed the whole story of why, when, how, and where.

The misadventure had taken place as Dave and four friends packed up camping gear and set out for California. The boys journeyed as far as the woods, three miles from home, before settling for the night. One boy's mother suspected their whereabouts, found the campsite, and confiscated about a thousand dollars worth of sleeping bags, tents, and backpacks. The boys had gone to the store for supplies (candy bars and gum). She imagined they'd scurry home upon discovering their missing stuff. She was wrong.

Would you slink back into town if you ran away and lost your parents' expensive gear—all in one night? They didn't. Instead, the boys searched till dawn. Ron picked them up on a back road about 8:00 A.M., dog-tired and near-panic.

"I sure prayed about that camping stuff. I thought it was stolen," Dave sighed, relieved to find his gear piled on our living-room floor.

I gathered up all my available strength and overcame my anger and hostility. Instead of saying, "How could you do this to us?" I hugged him and said, "Dave, I love you." Then added, "But why in the world would you want to run away from home?"

With glassy eyes, he shrugged his shoulders, headed for his bedroom, and collapsed for twenty-four hours.

Why, indeed? I don't understand why any kid would want to leave the comfort and security of home. Sure, I realize some parents abuse their children and trouble in the home is paramount. In those families, home is the pits; but most of us parents live from day to day, hoping our kids won't abuse *us*.

We've never used cruel and unusual punishment (by parental standards). Our kids have always had food (when they'd eat it), clothes, and a lot of love. In spite of all this, our son decided there existed a better place than home.

"Didn't you ever want to get away from your parents?" Dave asked during our family discussion about the runaway matter.

"Well, sometimes. I stayed at Grandma and Grandpa's a lot," I admitted.

"See!"

"Yes, Dave, I see. So stay at Grandma's sometimes, but don't run away from home."

COMPLIANT CARYL GROWS RESTLESS

While Dave still nurses the urge to leave home, Caryl on the other hand, hasn't seemed particularly interested in leaving. Perhaps she learns her lessons well from the escapades of her older brother. She likes it here—most of the time.

How nice of God to supply us with these opposites. Satan's work in guilt building would be monumental if both kids had decided home was a place to run away from. I felt guilty enough, wondering what we had done to force Dave's evacuation.

It was Caryl who convinced me it wasn't my fault. She assured me her brother was simply confused about the meaning of independence and freedom. In her words, "David's just weird."

Caryl, up to this point, has been one of those easy growers. At fifteen, she is sensitive and caring.

Perfect? No, but her transition through adolescence leans more toward tranquil than storm-tossed. Having a compliant child is like a dryer-warm blanket on a wintry night. It's like finding a familiar face in a crowd of sixty thousand strangers.

I certainly hope the easy growing continues. Fact is, I already see signs of restlessness. She talks and writes and giggles with and about boys. Secret notes and letters flow in and out of the house with such fervor, I'm thinking of opening my own mail distribution center. I'd save money over the stamps I buy.

Lately she's taken an interest in books like *Ice Castles, The Summer of the Sky-Blue Bikini,* and *Love Comes to Ann.* I wonder how long the tranquility will reign between us.

The thought of her dating has my stress level racing, as I anticipate floor pacing, stomach-churning anxiety over that first date. Worry, guilt, and fear will, I'm sure, pour in and boil over on that inevitable day. Even though I know what's coming, I don't know if I can stop the attack.

My only defense is to think of my daughter's future in positives instead of falling into a negative trap again. God will give me the strength to get through whatever lies ahead. Most important, I'll make certain she knows I love her—unconditionally.

Oh ... that reminds me. You know what she said the other day? "Mom, you love David more than me, don't you?"

I couldn't believe it. After all my efforts toward unlimited, unconditional love, how could she accuse me of such a thing? "Of course not," I reassured. "What makes you think that?"

"Well, you're always worried about him. He gets all the attention."

"It doesn't have anything to do with how much I love *you*. I love you both. The difference has to do with condition."

"Condition?"

"Yes. The condition I'm in. You see, when things are going okay and you guys are both behaving, I feel good, like being wrapped in a warm blanket. I can reach out and wrap you in love. When something goes wrong, like when Dave ran away, I feel like I'm hanging onto a cliff in an earthquake. It's hard to reach out and love somebody when you're afraid to let go."

"I see what you mean, but I still feel left out."

"Maybe, when you feel that way, and you can see me worried and hanging on, if you come and hug me, we can start feeling better together."

She has, and we do.

ARE THE KIDS DEPARENTING ME?

Caryl's response to my feelings has impressed me. If I am honest about my concerns and tell my children why I feel insecure about deparenting, will it help? With nothing to lose except inhibitions, I tried it.

I can see a change. I can't be sure, but I think they are trying to deparent *me* a little more gradually. Lately, I have to admit, release is easier. Dave and Caryl are showing all the signs of growing up. Sometimes watching them grow is fun. I actually relax and loosen my hold, give them a few more yards of rope, and pray they won't hang themselves. Seriously, I *can* see signs of progress.

For example, over the last six months, Dave has made two surprising advances. One, he stayed home for a weekend alone, and we and the house survived. Two, I caught him reading *U.S. News & World Report* and *National Geographic* magazine a few weeks ago. When asked why, he casually replied, "It's interesting." Not long after that enlightening intellectual revolution, he courteously left us a page-and-a-half note, telling us where he'd gone and when to expect him back. He proceeded to add a couple of jokes and a compliment. We're having it framed.

The independence Dave desires is close. Just the other day, Dave shocked me with the statement, "Brian and me are moving into an apartment as soon as I get a job."

My first response was to cry. My second, to say, "You're too young." However, I wisely gathered my parental strength, tried to understand his strong desire to be on his own, and said, "That sounds like a good plan. Before you go, we'll have to sit down together and talk about budgeting. That includes little things such as how to shop for groceries and still have enough money left to pay the rent."

Knowing how strong his quest for independence is, I expected him to tell me that he and Brian already knew how to handle it. Instead, he nodded his head and said, "Good idea, Mom. Thanks!" (Another entry for my journal.)

To be honest, I'm hoping when he learns how much money and time it takes to run a household, he'll decide home is better, at least until he graduates. But, if he does leave, at least he'll be well equipped. And, an extra bonus for me is (*chuckle*) the lessons will hold him still for a few minutes, so I can talk with him.

As you deparent, your children are allowed more and more independence. But when you hit the teenage years, the deparenting process seems to run with breakneck speed. In order to be ready for and to survive these fast moving years, you'll need those six strategies in hand and available for instant use.

One of the most useful strategies during the independence era is *love*. Love doesn't mean you must smother your child into dependency, until you're ready to let go. Rather, love is teaching your teenager how to get along on his or her own. Love your kids enough to let them go.

Many parents I talk to feel totally deparented already, because their teenagers are so seldom around. We'll take a closer look at these vanishing teens in chapter 11.

HOW TO FEEL GOOD ABOUT LETTING GO

1. Develop friendships with people who have successfully deparented and who will disclose their secrets. (Beware of the ideal "never had a problem" parent, however.)

2. *Be firm.* Don't let your teenagers' push for independence drive you to letting them go before you feel they are ready. They may still need rules and guidelines. While backing down to their demands may be easier at the time, the long-term results could be disastrous. It may leave you feeling guilty with "if onlys."

3. Remind yourself that this pulling away from parental control is a normal process—natural and healthy. The struggle comes in how much and how soon to let go. Each family is different, so establish deparenting guidelines best suited for your home (and each individual child).

4. Make a list of all the responsibilities required to lead a so-called independent life. Tell them as soon as they accomplish

everything on the list, they'll be ready. Take care you don't make the list too complicated; they may never want to leave.

5. Pray for wisdom to know each of your child's needs for both freedom and restriction.

11

The Disappearing Teen

Along with the push for independence in the teenager comes the problem of increasing absence from home. Thus, your latest questions might be, "How do I parent or *de*parent my teenagers when, half the time, I can't find them?"

That is a problem. The fact is, even when you do find them, communication often falters. Psychologists and counselors encourage, "Communicate with your teenagers." Dr. Haim Ginott even advocates that we learn a new language so we can speak to our kids on *their* level, in *their* way.

That would be nice but not realistic. I'm fairly well convinced that our children, at least, wouldn't want Ron and me to know. If we did manage to break the code, I'm sure they'd set up a new one.

I'D LIKE TO TALK TO MY KIDS BUT ...

Actually, we do communicate—whenever they are around. I must admit we do it with different degrees of success.

Sometimes Dave and Caryl communicate with angry looks,

or perhaps the silent treatment, when I have to say something like, "No, you can't go to the movies." Other times they communicate a word or two they shouldn't. At moments like that, I would like to communicate back with a punch in the mouth.

Occasionally, we have good days, and they even smile. On rare occasions we even have talks. I like to talk with my children. Problem is, they don't often want to talk with me. If, by chance, we happen to come in contact long enough to toss a few words around, the conversation usually flows in the direction of:

"Mom, I need a new pair of Nikes."

"You owe me twenty bucks—pay up."

"I haf'ta bring six-dozen cookies to church today."

When they want to talk, it's usually to ask for something. Then *I* feel like rebelling, "Hey, kids," I want to say, "I'm your mother, not your slave."

Once in a while, I wish they'd talk with me about their lives, and what they feel is important. I can't believe all they ever have on their minds is shoes, money, clothes and "Can I have the car?"

A friend of mine has a similar problem. In seeking a deeper relationship with her teenage son, she asked a youth counselor for help. At his suggestion, she asked her son, "What are your interests? Are you having any particular problems I can help you with?"

He remarked, "It's none of your business."

Heartbroken, she cries, "He doesn't want me to be a part of his life."

She needed uplifting. "Kathy," I told her, "If I asked my kids a direct question like that, I'd get the same answer. Believe me, I know how you feel."

"But you don't seem disturbed by it. Doesn't it bother you?"

"Of course. But I've taken to gleaning."

"Gleaning?"

"Right. I listen close to everything they say. Once in a while they slip up and let me in on their secret thoughts and desires. I've learned a lot about what they think by listening to what they don't say. Like most people, their actions and tone of voice gives them away."

Kathy wasn't ecstatic when I left, but she agreed to give it another try. "He's my son; I love him, and I'm a part of his life whether he likes it or not."

What's a rejected parent to do? Spy? Conversations with a teenager can be as nonproductive as arguing with a computer; but at least the computer has a legible readout.

BREAKING THE SECRECY BARRIER

Dave is one teenager who immensely enjoys his secrecy and prides himself in telling me no more than is absolutely necessary. I often end up playing Sherlock Holmes, as I rely on secondhand information about him and his activities. Fortunately, I usually get positive feedback such as, "We enjoyed having Dave spend the night. He has a great personality, and what a sense of humor."

The personality change between home and away from home reminds me of my own teenage years. Around town I was known as "Miss Personality"; but at home I didn't bubble much—in fact, I foamed. Some of my friends see this same basic pattern in their own children and wonder if they can communicate with anyone. Fortunately, by doing a little detective work, they soon find out from others that their youngsters *can* be civil and even entertaining.

Lately, I've been making a concentrated effort to get to know my children, despite their concerted efforts to ignore me. I watch them react around others and try to assure them, "Hey, I love you as you really are. I'd be willing to forgo reality for a few short skits of 'Mr. Nice Guy.' It's all right to show off your sparkling personalities at home. I could handle it. In light of what I did to *my* folks, I don't deserve it; but I could handle it."

I remember when the children were little. They used to chatter all the time—incessantly. I wished they'd saved a little for now. Over the years, the talking dwindled. I started feeling remorse over the lack of communication. All the books said, "Keep the lines of communication open between you and your teenagers." They were closing, and guilt moved in.

THE TEENAGE EVADER STRIKES AGAIN

Not long ago I experienced one of my biggest failures as communicator. Communication with my then-sixteen-year-old Dave had practically ceased. I decided that in order to keep guilt under control and open the communication lines again, I'd better whip out my strategy arsenal. Positive thinking, humor, and love would serve as my strongest weapons. With my strategies in mind, I set out to crash through the communication barrier between my teenage son and me. It wouldn't be an easy task.

Dave began to develop his avoidance skills on his twelfth birthday, and by sixteen he was an expert. He became as elusive as the money in my bank account, and as flitting as the tooth fairy. He cunningly sidestepped confrontations with adults—especially his parents, unless he needed cash, food, wheels, or someone to hem up his jeans.

I knew it was time for a chat. I'd been meaning to discuss several matters with him. Aside from falling behind in his school work, Dave's crammed schedule barely left time for meals. The last time we sat down to dinner, he inhaled his food and headed out the door before the *n* sounded on *amen.* I yearned to get reacquainted with my son and determined to catch up with him that day, between school and gymnastics practice. Who knows? Maybe I'd get lucky and observe, firsthand, one of his growth spurts.

He won't escape this time, I chuckled ruthlessly. *The minute he opens the door, I'll nab him and hold him captive, until I've said everything I've wanted to say to him for the past four years.*

I looked forward to an uninterrupted, pleasant conversation with my transient teenager.

At 2:00 P.M. the front door slammed. "Hi, Dave!" I cheerfully greeted from the living-room couch, where I had already made myself comfortable for our talk. "How was school? Have any homework?"

From the hallway came a faint groan, which I promptly took for *hello.* "Nope, no homework. Can I go over to Adam's?"

"Not right now. Come in here and sit down. I want to talk with you about something."

Silence.

"Dave?" I called out, feeling mysteriously alone. Had I actually talked to someone just then, or was it my imagination? Had I been foiled? Had the Teenage Evader struck again?

The slam of another door echoed from the end of the hall—his bedroom. The muscles in my neck tightened, while a little voice inside me advised, *"Don't get angry. Maybe he didn't hear you. Be calm. Good mothers don't lose their tempers."* I drew in a deep breath, squared my shoulders and walked stiffly down the hall, straining to keep my composure.

I grabbed for the knob, about to make my entrance, when the bold fluorescent letters plastered all over his door reprimanded me.

BEWARE! KNOCK BEFORE ENTERING! ENTER AT YOUR OWN RISK . . . THIS MEANS YOU!

I quickly withdrew my hand from the knob, then leaned my ear to the door and knocked gently. "Dave, I want to talk to you." Tension crept into my voice.

"Can't it wait, Mom? I've got. . . ." His last words were obliterated as the blare of rock music blasted my ears.

"What did you say?" I yelled over the shrieking sounds, which now vibrated the floor beneath me. "Turn that thing down! Are you deaf?"

"It's not loud. I can hardly hear it," he argued, obediently turning the music down about half-a-decibel. "I'm doing my homework."

"Lord," I whispered through gritted teeth, "if there is any joy in this, You'd better show me, 'cause I sure can't see it." A surge of adrenalin permeated my body; every muscle tightened. *Take it easy, stay calm,* my little voice preached. I wish, just once, my adrenal gland and my little voice would agree on something.

Straining to keep my voice pleasant, I replied, "But you said you didn't have any."

"I forgot. I've got to do a term paper by tomorrow."

"Come out, anyway," I insisted. "This is important. I want to talk to you. And turn that thing off, I'm tired of competing with it."

This encounter had fast become a battle of wills. I'd forgotten what I wanted to discuss with him. No matter. I would not let him off the hook. Dave was going to talk to me, if I had to tie him down and sit on him.

"Do you want me to flunk? It's gonna take me all night to get this paper done, and if I don't, I'll flunk history."

More determined than ever, I persisted. "The homework will have to wait. This won't take long." A lump formed in my throat. *What do I say if he opens the door? I'll think of something. After all, I'm his mother. Mothers always have words of wisdom. This is ridiculous. Why am I getting so upset about talking to my own son?*

The music stopped. Grudgingly, Dave opened the door and leaned his muscular five-feet-four-inch frame against the doorjamb—at last, face to face, mother and son. "Well, wha' d' ya want?" came his disdainful reply.

I groaned silently, as I realized the main purpose for this urgent discussion was his neglected homework. I wish I could have disappeared, as Dave had done earlier.

Dave's blue-green eyes melted away my anger and frustration of the last few minutes.

What could I do?

I leaned forward and gave him a big hug, kissed his cheek and humbly replied, "I love you." Placing my hands on his broad shoulders, I turned him around and gave him a gentle shove. "Go do your homework." I could tell by his grin, he thought he'd won.

With the door closed once again, I murmured, "Oh, well, maybe he'll need his jeans hemmed tomorrow."

I suppose if you were to rate my parental effectiveness on that one, you might give me a two on a scale of one to ten. Once again, it didn't look like I came off as a very strong parent, one of the strategies I've been working on for years. Maybe you'd be right, but nonetheless, I'd still give myself an eight for that encounter. I didn't lose my cool and as far as I'm concerned, that took phenomenal strength. Besides, a hug and kiss are excellent communicators of love. He did his homework, and finally, I even had the opportunity to rejoice. It really was a funny scene.

Actually, I'd have scored myself a ten, but I lost two points on guilt. Yes, *guilt.* I couldn't help myself. Almost immediately, guilt's grip tightened. I struggled to find the reason why my son and I can't talk to each other.

WHY CAN'T WE TALK?

Why is it so hard for me to talk with my son? Other people like to talk with me, so I know it can't be my breath or boredom. I tell him a joke, he tells me "it's dumb." I tell him he can go to the movies after he's begged me for an hour, then he doesn't want to go. He's the only person I know who can turn a smile into a fist fight.

Why can't we talk? Maybe he's too young for a formal conversation. Am I expecting too much of my sixteen-year-old? Is his attention span too short? That's crazy. Anyone with a short attention span couldn't spend four hours on the phone with one girl.

Experienced parents tell me it's normal for teenagers to oppose their parents and willfully avoid communication. Diminished conversation with parents is part of the rebellion in the fight for independence. I'm convinced two of the declarations in their by-laws must read:

- Never let parents think they are right.
- Never say more than three or four words in a civil tone, at any given time, to a parent or you'll be charged with treason.

As a conversationalist with my teenagers, I admit, I'm no William Buckley. As long as I keep my mouth shut and let them spout off about unfairness, cruelty, injustice, and liberty for all (except parents), they'll talk to me. The minute I defend my actions or beliefs, object, give advice or even give my opinion, the conversation ends. But, not until I've been duly accused, *"Mother,* you never listen. You just don't understand."

It's true, I don't understand. I don't understand how I could have reared children who can't listen to a second opinion, when said opinion is from the mouth of a parent. I don't understand why they don't understand me.

What did I do wrong? I hang my head in shame, wounded and filled with guilt.

How can I overcome this feeling of inadequacy and negative thinking?

Just as I was ready to self-destruct and end up in the dumps for good, I decided to call in reinforcements. I quickly dialed my friend Lauraine. "I need help. I started thinking about how my kids won't talk with me and guilt has gotten a stifling hold."

"Pull up!" commanded my strong friend. "Think! When was the last good conversation you had with the kids?"

"Hmmm ..." I thought for a moment. "Last week, during a Bible study. Dave presented the passage. I knew he wasn't prepared, because he flipped open the Book and started reading. His face took on a pained expression, as he realized he'd picked the Old Testament. Uncharted territory. 'Hosea 9:1–4: Rejoice not, O Israel! Exult not like the peoples; for you have played the harlot, forsaking your God. You have loved a harlot's hire upon all the threshing floors. ...' He struggled through the text.

"When he finished, he slapped the pages of the Book together, chewed on his lip, and slowly nodded his head, as if in deep thought. He looked first at the floor, then lifted his eyes to meet ours. Then he spoke.

" 'There's *gotta* be a lesson in there somewhere.' His bold, theological statement sent tension flying and brought streams of laughter. When we finally settled down, we had one of the best studies ever."

"You're doing better," continued the strong, positive voice of my parent-friend. "Another one quick."

"Ah.... Oh, yes. Just the other day Caryl and I had a touching and revealing 'mother-daughter' talk. I'd been wanting to share some experiences and personal thoughts. I wanted to know about her plans and ideas on dating and boy-girl relationships. We ended our conversation with tears and hugs. I think we understand each other more."

I felt a flood of release. Guilt's power diminished in the light of positive reinforcements. "It's working Lauraine. I ... I'll be all right now. Thanks."

"You're sure?"

"Yes. You know how negative thoughts can build up and out of proportion. How can I repay you?"

"Just keep your head straight and do the same for me or another wounded parent sometime."

After we hung up, I felt refreshed. There have been good times. My journal proves that. My kids don't *always* ignore me. I'm a loving, sensitive, caring parent-person. I love my children. It's not my fault they choose not to talk to me sometimes.

A SURE-FIRE WAY TO COMMUNICATE

When teenagers choose to be silent, there isn't much a parent can do. However, in order to maintain a healthy distance away from exaggerated guilt, worry, anxiety and fear, I've developed my own sure-fire system of communication.

If I don't accomplish anything else as a parent, my children are going to know I love them. Everyday, as you know, I hug my kids (if I can find them) and say, "I love you." Consequently, according to my theory, I am doing my part to communicate that all-important message to their brains. Since I make such a point of hugs and "love yous," they would have to conclude either I do love them or I'm illiterate and those are the only words I know.

Not all lack of communication is the fault of the children. Sometimes a quick hug and love is all any of us has time for or can think of. Our fast-paced world annihilates conversations. Not only does "fast living" cut communication between parents and teenagers, but between husbands and wives and others. Seminars pop up all over the place to improve lines of communication for everyone.

Because of our rush-rush-hurry-up attitudes, we often transmit verbal and nonverbal messages. "I don't have time"; or "I need my space—stay clear."

Of course, I can't forget the greatest communication canceler of all—*television.*

Our bodies and minds no longer accept quiet times and relaxing atmospheres. Everytime I take a break or go for a walk, my guilty conscience convinces me I'm lazy and have too much work to do. My worrywart mind has me thinking, *If you keep goofing off, you'll never meet your deadline.*

Busy people, running people—lonely people. In our home, between gymnastics practice, school, sporting events, and work, we're lucky to sit down to dinner together twice a week. Today I prepared a gourmet dinner. Six-thirty, no one's home but me. Guess I'll have to eat alone. Where'd everybody go?

Ever try to communicate with an artichoke?

COPING AND COMMUNICATING WITH THE DISAPPEARING TEENAGER

1. Try disappearing at dinner (without making it). They'll probably tear the house apart trying to find you.

2. Purchase a pair of handcuffs and cuff the listener of your choice to the bed before wakeup time. Then talk.

3. Jot down successful conversations in a journal as ammunition for when you've convinced yourself of failure.

4. Have the phone number of a parent-sharing partner close at hand, in case you need help.

5. Talk to your spouse or close friend frequently. This will assure you that you have not lost the ability to converse.

6. Take time! Take time to *know* and *hug* and *love* your teenager.

12

The Food Game

"Gross! Oh, no! Mom, not green beans in the spaghetti sauce." Dismayed, disgruntled, and distressed, Dave stormed out of the kitchen. "I'm not gonna' eat that junk. You ruined it. Spaghetti's my favorite. Why 'ja hafta wreck it?"

That was the longest oration I'd heard from my sixteen-year-old in months. I was in no mood, however, to discuss the merits of an all-inclusive diet, so I settled for a few words. "Fine, the less you eat, the more I save on the food bill."

To further thwart his untantalized taste buds, I proceeded to cook cauliflower on which to pour the bean-laden Italian meat sauce. Delicious!

My guilt complex, being what it is, however, I felt compelled to boil up a side dish of noodles. And so, both kids enjoyed the dinner after straining out the beans. I'm sure they considered me a turncoat for my actions.

"What are you trying to do, Mom, start trouble?" Dave reprimanded between mouthfuls. "If you want us to eat, you've got to fix foods we like."

"Sure, I want you to eat, but I have an imagination, and I can't stand to cook the same foods day after day, week after week, simply to satisfy your finicky appetites."

"You keep this up, and I'll just have to eat somewhere else."

"I'm simply trying to provide my family with well-balanced meals, Dave, and using more vegetables, whole grains, and less meat is my plan of action."

"I liked the food here better before you got carried away on this health-food kick. I even like liver."

"Vegetables, kids, we have to eat more vegetables."

"Then I guess we'll have to eat less," came the consensus from the teenage representatives.

EVERYBODY PLAYS THE FOOD GAME

Eat less! G-R-O-A-N. If your mind runs anywhere in the same direction as mine, you find food and the teenager problem wide open to our potentially detrimental emotions. Worry and guilt win the race in the food game.

I read somewhere that teenagers need as many as four thousand calories a day, just to maintain their present weight. During adolescence their bodies grow faster than at any other time, except infancy.

My mathematically genius mind quickly calculated that if my kids continue to eat at their present intake, they would return to infancy by 1995 to 1997. Needless to say, my guilt soared. How are they going to get the food they need?

"You don't eat enough to keep a bird alive," I complain to my Olive Oyl daughter. The only foods my teenagers eat too much of are snacks. Then, believe it or not, I actually tell them,

"If you keep stuffing your face with that junk food, you'll get fat." Frankly, I'm jealous. They never gain an extra pound. I do.

Guilt creeps up on me when I prepare nutritional meals, and they don't eat them. Since they're gone so much of the time, with their full schedules, I worry that they won't stop to eat. Something's got to give. I cannot spend the rest of my days, worrying about what they eat. What to do? Think positive.

The only positive thing I could think of is that if they don't eat, I should be able to save as much as 20 percent on our grocery bill.

With my new attitude of nonworry, I could blurt out nonchalant comments like, "If you don't like what I fix, don't eat." Sometimes, though, guilt and sympathy compelled me to do a few reruns of meat, corn, potatoes, and gravy, or cook extra side dishes of their favorite foods. I thought, generally, if I provided a good variety of foods, they'd eat enough to balance out eventually. Not true.

For years I taught them about nutrition. "If you don't eat your vegetables, your bones will get soft, and you'll end up walking like rubber bands."

They would just laugh at me; now they won't even listen. I don't know how they manage to stay healthy. Truth is, they are more active, slimmer and trimmer than I am. Maybe I should start eating like them. Yuk! Never! Their choice of food has no class.

No, on the contrary, I've decided to ignore their unlimited or inhibited appetites and plunge into the world of gourmet cooking—health-food style. There are recipes I'd only dreamed of during all those drab, unimaginative meals.

Now, I torture my teenagers regularly with dishes like "Bulgar Pilaf" or my very own Stir-fried Veggies a la Smoked Oysters. This stir-fry recipe is recommended only for those seasoned cooks who are endowed with the ability to ignore cruel jokes a dish like this might bring.

"Are you trying to poison us?"

"I think I'm going to throw up."

"I'm fasting."

Ignore them. It's delicious! Go ahead and prepare *your* specialty. They may even like it.

WAS IT SOMETHING I FED THEM?

Although the kids lacked exceeding joy over my new cooking style, Ron and I ate better than ever. For the first time in years, I had the courage to prepare asparagus spears, with *real* hollandaise sauce, sprinkled liberally with toasted, slivered almonds. Yumm, yumm.

In spite of my health-food rebellion and tastier meals, at least from Ron's and my viewpoint, unsettled guilt continued to rise to the surface over the development of my children's eating patterns. Had I contributed to the problem when they were young and impressionable? I knew I had to resolve this complex once and for all.

I remember when they were babies. Every time I tried to feed the little rug rats their veggies, meat, or anything but fruit, cereal, and milk, their little pink tongues pushed it out and their tiny noses wrinkled in objection. I probably shouldn't have mixed fruit with the cereal, or offered fruit before vegetables. Oh, but then I committed the unforgivable sin. I added corn syrup to their formula. A sugar pusher—I got my kids addicted.

Luckily, I caught myself before I slipped deeper into guilt. It wasn't my idea to feed my babies milk and fruit first. The *doctor* told me to.

Now that they're grown, I certainly don't encourage my teenagers to choose Big Macs, hotdogs, pizzas, and tacos instead of my nutritious meals. Can I help it if they have poor taste?

Poor taste or not, one of my goals as a parent is to provide a balanced diet for my family. I guess they'll have to worry about their own bodies. I'm certain they'll grow, regardless of how and what they eat now.

Still, I sought answers. I decided maybe I should change my priorities slightly. "What can I do to get the right kinds of food into my kids?" I asked myself. Well, I started reading.

Some of the earlier books suggested we let them eat what they want. "They'll just naturally go for what's good for them." Horsefeathers! I tossed that book aside. Apparently, the author had never run into a "passive-resistive" child. Caryl developed a routine which rarely ceased to foil us. She diverted our attention by gabbing. She would talk about how good the food was, about school, the weather, or anything. The conversations were so pleasant, we forgot about the food and didn't notice until cleanup time, her plate was still full.

I tried the coaxing and threatening with no dessert, but that didn't work either.

I ran across an article in *Families,* published by *Reader's Digest.* The article (from the May 1981 issue) "Feeding Your Fast Food Freaks," discussed the teenagers' eating habits. "Erratic eating habits are normal among adolescents, and no amount of wheedling, nagging, scolding or threatening will get teenagers back into the family fold when it comes to food."

What a relief. My teenagers are normal. At least that's what I thought until I read further. Then, I wondered if maybe our family was an anomaly. "Leftovers such as fish cakes, meat loaf, chicken, boiled or roasted potatoes, stir-fried green beans and steamed broccoli (a delicious snack when eaten cold with vinaigrette or Italian dressing) will be gobbled up by a foraging adolescent with a voracious appetite, much to his or her nutritional benefit."

They've got to be kidding. Ron or I might find those leftovers appealing, but not my children. Oh, the chicken or meat maybe—but *broccoli? Fish cakes? Meat loaf?* Mention stir-fry beans and my kids go into hysterics.

I guess some people are lucky, or they did something right early on. I have met only one child who would eat anything.

My six-year-old niece Shanna. She's an angel—eats everything. She even enjoyed my stir-fried vegetables and asked for seconds.

"SO, SEND IT TO CHINA!"

My reading project didn't fail completely. In fact, once I started reading books like *Living More with Less* and the *More-with-Less Cookbook,* both by Doris Longacre; *Diet for a Small Planet* by Frances M. Lappe; and *The Supper of the Lamb* by Robert F. Capon, my whole concept of food and eating changed.

I had been brought up with the knowledge that there were people in the world who had nothing to eat and we should all be thankful for our bountiful blessings. "Clean your plate. We don't want to waste our food. There are people starving in China," my mother would tell me. So I told my kids. Funny, I never could figure out why my eating more would help someone who was hungry.

Yet, this theory to encourage kids to eat must be used by mothers all over the world. A young man from China once told me, "My mother used to say, 'Eat your rice, son. There are people starving in West Virginia.' " Even though the lesson runs worldwide, I'm afraid it doesn't work any better than other methods for convincing kids to eat right. My children would simply retort back with "So send it to them."

My consciousness moved from worrying about my children, because they shared in the resources and bountiful supplies of food, to the starving population of the world. I came to the conclusion that our eating habits are closely related to our selfish desires. We eat to satisfy our insatiable appetites. We usually eat by habit, whether we're hungry or not. I'd never been truly hungry and neither had my children.

I felt a gnawing pang of guilt, and this time it wasn't false guilt, but a conviction from God. I knew our family ate more food and possessed more material goods than we needed. My strategy in the food game I played with my children changed drastically. My new motto is "Live simply so others may simply live."

I wanted my family to be aware of the critical situations in our world. I wanted them to be willing to sacrifice for the well-being of others. As you may have observed at the beginning of the chapter, Dave and Caryl didn't take kindly to the changes. Less red meat, more lentils, and the introduction of soy. . . . They were open to some of the changes and have yet to detect the more subtle substitutions in their favorite foods. I've become an expert in the art of sneaking good stuff into their junk food, as well as regular meals.

Wheat germ disguises itself easily in waffles, pancakes, and sauces. Milkshakes and juices become richer and more nutritional with a raw egg blended in. My kids love the addition. I toss lentils and barley into homemade soups, and once in a while the kids accidently swallow a couple. My flour mixture, which is used for all baking and cooking is one-half wheat flour and one-half unbleached. Pureed vegetables, even the ones the kids refuse, end up as stock in stews. What they don't know can make them healthier.

While my concern is still to provide nutritious meals, I have learned that more is not necessarily better. I've also learned that meals do not have to be served three times a day, seven days a week.

Our family joined with friends, about sixty-five in all, and participate in a day we call "Potato Day." On Thursday supper, we eat baked potatoes with margarine, salt and pepper and water. The money saved over the cost of a normal meal is sent to Bread for the World, an organization of Christians united against world hunger and poverty. My children are partakers in an effort to feed the hungry. Our prayer for the simple evening meal is:

"POTATO DAY" PRAYER

Lord, at the beginning of this simple meal
we turn to You.

We are reminded of the multitudes in other
lands, as well as in our own, who would find . . .
    this warm meal a feast,
    this warm place a palace,
    this caring community a miracle.
We do not know how to cope with their need nor the
structures that cause hunger and hardship for so many . . .
but, we pause in the midst of the normal pattern of our
week to remember the hungry. And by this small token,
to suffer with them and to become sensitive to ways in
which we can share the resources of Your world with all
Your beloved creation.

Amen.

NORMA KNUTSON
Golden Valley, Minnesota

Can you imagine *me,* Number One Guilt-ridden Mother *encouraging* her teenagers to forgo a full-course meal and eat only potatoes? Miracles never cease. Comments about Potato Day from my kids are "It's a good idea"; "Everybody should do it."

Many of our Potato Day friends also participate in a fast day. Usually, we choose to fast together for twenty-four to thirty-six hours; that is, from evening meal of one day to evening meal the next. I used to think my children would never survive a day without food. Now I understand that a day or two of fasting is not only physically healthy but spiritually beneficial as well. The money saved from these fast days is also sent to "Bread for the World."

Food and feeding my family has finally been placed in the right perspective. I no longer suffer guilt and worry over their eating or lack of eating. My concern (and, hopefully, the concern of my children) has turned to those who have no food. Our food is a gift from God. Overeating or overconcern to satisfy insatiable appetites is a greed suffered by many in our prosperous nation.

WHAT'S YOUR FOOD-GAME STRATEGY?

In playing the food game, parents would do well to ask, "Just what do I want to teach my children?" For Ron and me, it is awareness of their actual bodily needs, and, we'd like them to develop a moral and social consciousness.

Another point I'd like to make in discussing this food game is this: our likes and dislikes for food usually change as we mature. I used to detest practically every form of vegetable. Now I can't get my fill. I'm sure all of us at one time or another have gone through periods of erratic eating patterns, when our nutritional needs were neglected. Most of us haven't fared too poorly. There *are* worse problems than baldness and soft fingernails.

Perhaps before I close this chapter, I should say a few words of caution about the child who develops a chronic or severe eating problem. Extreme weight gain or loss can be symptoms of serious underlying psychological problems. Symptoms of obesity or anorexia nervosa should be discussed with a physician. This is not a problem parents should try to handle alone.

Most teenagers won't fall into the chronic category, so, if you're a parent who has stirred up guilt and worry over your teenager's eating habits, *relax.* They'll eventually outgrow it. There are many more important projects you can throw your energies into. Just remember, if your children aren't concerned about nutrition now, watch them move when they start feeding your grandchildren.

WINNING THE FOOD GAME

1. Determine to provide nourishing meals and leave the eating of them up to the individual.

2. Develop a moral and social consciousness regarding world hunger and poverty.

3. Place a poster or two in your home suggesting a "Live more simply for the benefit of others" theme.

4. Suggest a planned famine for your local youth group. There is such a program available through World Vision International. The young people are all involved in a thirty-hour fast titled "Let it Growl." Participants may purchase a T-shirt with a growling, hungry lion printed on the front. Through this program of viewing films on world hunger and feeling empty tummies, they can share "the hunger experience of 65 percent of the world's population who go to bed hungry every night." Other ideas available by writing to: World Vision International

Box O, Pasadena, California 91109

5. Pray for understanding of the Lord's words, "Man shall not live by bread alone . . ." (Matthew 4:4). ". . . for I was hungry and you gave me food, I was thirsty and you gave me drink, I was a stranger and you welcomed me, I was naked and you clothed me, I was sick and you visited me, I was in prison and you came to me." Then the righteous will answer him, "Lord when did we see thee hungry and feed thee, or thirsty and give thee drink? And when did we see thee a stranger and welcome thee, or naked and clothe thee? And when did we see thee sick or in prison and visit thee?" And the King will answer them, "Truly, I say to you, as you did it to one of the least of these my brethren, you did it to me." (Matthew 25:35–40)

6. Use your strategies.

- *Strength* and a *positive attitude* play the food game and win.
- A foundation of *love* reaches you and your family out to "love your neighbor as yourself."
- *Authenticity* and *sensitivity to suffering* touches you with the real world . . . a hungry world . . . a hurting world.
- *Joy* helps others.

13

The Driving Force

At sixteen years of age, according to the average teenager, it's time to drive—time to drive their very own car, the family car (or, in truth), to drive their parents crazy.

It's not too difficult to get your mind off their poor eating habits once the driving starts. The guilt and worry you may have had over whether or not they eat, quickly turns to anxiety and fear, as you wonder if they'll ever survive the "Learn to Drive" experience.

CAR FEVER STRIKES WHEN LEAST EXPECTED

I'll never forget the first episode of "car fever." Of course, I suspected the driving force would emerge within the year, but when this new episode overtook Dave's life, it caught me totally unprepared. You see, Ron and I enjoyed several weeks of temporary truce. I guess I shouldn't have let the tranquility go to my head. In the middle of my false sense of security, Dave dropped his drive bomb.

He'd gone to visit a friend. A sharp *ring* brought me out of my utopian daydream, a world without cars—or telephones. "Hello."

"Mom, can I go roller skating?" a husky voice echoed over the line.

"Tonight? Dave, you're supposed to go to church tonight—Luther league, remember?"

"Ah, Mom. It's too boring. I never have fun there. Besides, Greg's my new friend and. . . ."

"Sorry," I interrupted. "I'm going to church too, so I can't drive you." (*What superb parental manipulation,* I thought proudly.)

"That's okay," his voice echoed, "Greg has a car. He'll drive."

My voice stuck in my throat, while my heart tried to escape. "A c-c-car?" I stammered. "Who is this kid anyway? How old is he? Isn't he a little too young to drive?"

"Mom, he's the same age I am, sixteen, remember? Most people do get their licenses when they're sixteen. Just because you and Dad wouldn't let me take driver's training this year."

"Well. . . . Personally, I think sixteen is too young."

"Mom, can I go roller skating?"

"Actually, no. You can't," my senses returned. "I'm giving the presentation on 'The Potter and the Clay' at your youth meeting tonight. Did you forget?"

"Ah, Mom, I've heard all your clay philosophies before. This is a chance of a lifetime."

Roller skating? A chance of a lifetime? This conversation was not going well at all. "Dave," I pleaded, "how can I face all those kids and convince them what I have to say is meaningful, when my own son won't go?"

"You can make it on your own, Mom. I have faith in you. Besides, I won't always be around you know."

Strength, I thought to myself. *I've got to stand my ground, but I'm beginning to weaken. Stall. Stall for time,* my brain wisely advised.

"Dave, why don't you come home, and we'll talk about it some more. Maybe you can go after the meeting. Bring your friend along to dinner."

The silence on the end of the line told me the compromise registered slightly less than acceptable.

"It's that or nothing," I asserted.

"Well, I'll be home after a while."

Relieved, I discussed the problem with Ron, and the two of us made a strong united front.

"You either go to church with your mom, or you forget the roller skating," Ron commanded with authority.

"Okay, but can Greg and me drive over to the church by ourselves and go skating from there?"

"Yes—that's okay," Ron agreed, "but be sure you stay for the whole program and be home by ten."

With the meeting over, I bid the boys good-bye, "Drive carefully. And, don't forget to be home by ten."

"Don't worry, Mom. You know Greg's a good driver. You watched him like a hawk all the way over here."

"I . . . I did *n*———. Of course I *did* notice that he drove normally, but I wasn't paying that much attention." Rats! Sometimes I think that kid knows me better than I know myself.

Once home, I nearly forgot my son was out on the streets with a teenage driver. But at 9:55 P.M., as though operating on a built-in alarm system, my stomach hurt. My brain discharged half a dozen messages:

"He's been in an accident."

"They've split for California."

"Why did I let him go?"

"I knew it, if only. . . ."

"I hope he has clean underwear." (My mom always told me to wear clean underwear, in case I ended up in the hospital. So I told my kids.)

"I'll never forgive myself."

At 10:05 P.M. a car pulled in our driveway. I'd responded to another false alarm.

I suppose you're wondering why hysterics practically superceded my good sense over a silly little driving incident. On the other hand, maybe you're not wondering why, but I'm going to tell you anyway. *Statistics.*

Accident Facts, 1981 edition, by the National Safety Council revealed these facts:

- 21.7 percent of all drivers in the nation are between 15 and 24 years of age. 9.8 percent under 20 and 11.9 from 20-24.

- This 21.7 percent of the drivers were involved in 36.6 percent of all motor vehicle accidents. That's over ⅓ of the accidents involving young people under 24.

According to the National Highway Traffic Safety Administration:

- Arrests of teenagers for drunken driving have tripled since 1960.
- Accidents still lead in the cause of death for 15- to 24-year-olds in this country.

Of course, it's no secret that insurance agencies consider drivers in these age brackets high risks. The insurance payments are bankrupting.

These statistics, along with daily visual aids, are responsible for my agitated state when it comes to the teenage driver.

"DO YOU WANT TO DRIVE OR DON'T YOU?"

Panicstricken as I was with statistics, the driving force now controlled my son. What could I do? The law in our state allows a driver's permit at fifteen and a half, a license at sixteen. According to Dave, he was already past his prime. He moved quickly from "friend with car" to "self-motivation."

Dave's next step up featured a driver's training class. Ron and I accepted the idea that he would drive, but we held him back as long as possible with requirements.

The first requirement was that he recognize driving as an earned privilege, not a *right*. The second, that if he maintain a *B* average, he could take Driver's Ed second semester. Our efforts, of course, were unappreciated.

"All the other kids I know have already taken the class. I'm in with the dumb ones and the younger kids," Dave accused.

"Do you want to drive or don't you?" We firmly stood our ground.

His urge to sit behind the wheel and operate one of our ve-

hicles prompted an improved attitude, grades, and general behavior. I thought we'd done everything right. Unfortunately, I
made the mistake of feeling smug about the way we handled
our son. I forgot to anticipate his "drive" for complete freedom.

You see, the force behind the magic words *drive* and *car*
compelled Dave through Driver's Education. First-time failure
of his driver's test thwarted his mania for a week. Then, with
grit and determination, he passed the test and took the prize. A
driver's license stamped TEMPORARY found its home in Dave's
back pocket. The world had been conquered—he thought.

We continued to exercise our methods of gradual deparenting. Unfair and inhibiting rule Number One: "Drive alone. No
passengers, except for parents, for one month." We added,
"You need the practice, and the concentration."

This rule was not accepted with a good deal of grace. Wait a
month? Unreasonable! "I passed my test. There's no law
against taking passengers."

"Do you want to drive or don't you?" It worked the first
time, maybe it would work again.

Since Dave had no vehicle and no means with which to buy
one, he accepted the sentence—temporarily.

I know a lot of parents who try to place restrictions on their
kids' driving. I'm not sure these restrictions or setbacks have
too much effect on today's teenage driver.

A doctor friend, who works in the clinic with me, shared, "I
set limitations. My son didn't pay any attention to my rules or
caution. Now, he can't drive at all. He drove himself out of cars
and insurance. In six months he managed to total three cars,
two of mine and one of his own. The insurance company made
me sign a waiver not to let him drive. I tried to warn him. Now,
it's out of my hands. Some kids insist on living life the hard
way. It's tough, but what can I do?"

Another friend, Jane, says, "We told Tim if he wanted to
drive, he would have to pay for the insurance. The minute he
turned sixteen, he got a job. At first we felt pleased at his re-

sponsible behavior. Unfortunately, 'car fever' attacked full force. He earned money to buy a car. The car, in turn, became his god, demanding gas, insurance, and repairs. Tim quit school in his sophomore year, and took a fulltime job, so he and his car could live happily ever after. Maybe we should have bought him a car. Maybe he'd still be in school."

"Jane," I spoke reassuringly, "it doesn't do you any good to feel guilty. Besides, could you afford to support Tim's car habit?"

"Well . . . no, we couldn't. I guess you're right."

Once a kid gets car fever . . . it's . . . it's nearly hopeless. The only cure is maturity. Insurance companies tell me it can last until the youngster is twenty-five! All I needed was more evidence to tell me teenagers and cars mean "hazardous driving conditions."

"I JUST HAD TO GET OUT!"

Every time Dave took the car out, I had an anxiety attack. As far as we knew, he'd obeyed our rules about "no passengers." One night, less than a week away from the completion of his month of soloing, our "no passengers" rule lost to the passion of car fever.

I'd come home from working the evening shift in the clinic. Dave and his friend Greg exchanged pleasantries with me. After a few minutes, I excused myself for bed, and suggested the boys do the same. They seemed unusually cooperative. *He's up to something,* I mused. Feeling slight guilt at the thought, I dismissed it as paranoid. It turned out to be intuition.

B-r-i-n-g-g-g . . . r-r-i-i-n-n-g-g-g-. The muffled sound of the phone jolted me from a half-sleep. Since Dave's bedroom is located beneath ours, just off the family room, the long-corded telephone usually finds its place beside Dave's bed. *Why isn't he answering?* I thought. Something's wrong! I felt a sharp pang in my stomach. *He's not here.* I grabbed my bathrobe and hurried downstairs. My suspicions confirmed—pillows instead of boys occupied the beds. A quick look out the window revealed a missing '72 Toyota.

"Lord, it's not fair. I'm too young for all this grief." I grabbed my positive journal and Bible and planted myself on the living room couch to wait—and pray:

> Lord, keep the boys safe, but . . . do me a big favor and give that kid a good case of guilt and a stomachache to go with his conscience. He deserves it.

Every car that passed drew me to the window. I never realized how busy the streets were at two in the morning. At about 2:30 A.M. the little Toyota slowed down and started to turn into the drive. *Something's wrong.* With lights out, the little car backed out and moved down the road. Angry and curious, I stepped out on the deck above our garage and driveway. As I watched, the little car turned around again and headed home. It gained speed. The driver cut the motor, as he turned it into our steep drive. With all the concentration on sneaking in, Dave forgot to cut the lights. Can you imagine his surprise as they spotlighted a bathrobed and barefooted mother? The car rolled uncooperatively back down to the street. I could almost hear a groan, as the engine turned on and the car moved to its stall in front of the garage.

"Mom, please don't tell Dad. I just had to get out."

"You know the rules Dave; no passengers," I firmly replied, as I escorted them inside.

"That's a stupid rule. And besides, there's no reason why I can't take someone in the car with me. Look, Greg went and nothing happened."

"You got caught. Was it worth it?"

"No. My stomach started hurting and I felt guilty, so we came home."

Hmmm . . . God does *answer prayers.*

"I won't do anything like this again, Mom. Please don't tell Dad."

"Dave, you took our car. He needs to know you abused your privileges."

The ax fell the next morning, as Ron pronounced his judgment. "No driving for a week and no passengers for another month."

Even with a minor setback, it wasn't long before Dave became a full-fledged passenger-carrying driver.

OH, WHAT A BATTERED FEELING

Once again, the peaceful life canceled the anxiety and fear of danger over the new driver. I felt better. I had even found a few parents whose teenage drivers were accident-free.

Mari, for example, told me her three daughters all drove, the oldest for five years. The only incident they'd had was a fender-bender in a parking lot.

Hurray, there's hope. That evening, as darkness descended, so did our spirits. Dave arrived home from gymnastics, and in a quiet voice announced, "Well, now I know how it feels to be the victim of a drunk driver."

"Honey, are you all right?" I jumped up to inspect my son more closely and hugged him in relief.

"Ya, I'm fine. This car came at me on my side of the road. He forced me in the ditch and before I knew what happened, this sign wiped out the side of the car."

"What about the other car? Did you get a license, or identification?" Ron asked.

"No, it was too dark. All I saw were headlights."

No witness, no driver, and no other car. All we had was one small Toyota with a long wide scar across the passenger side.

This wasn't the first trauma to befall the little car. Since Dave started driving, it's been living a battered life. The compact brown Toyota has been with us since it came into this country. It's driven us safely and securely for ten years, and all it's ever needed was a minor fender repair and a paint job. Now look at it. Is this any way to treat a foreigner?

In six months of driving, Dave has reduced us from a two to a one-and-a-half car family. One day the antenna mysteriously disappeared. Two hubcaps turned up missing-in-action. The car smells like it's been bombed with milk. And, if this weren't enough, the poor thing recently suffered from a *near miss*.

One morning, as Ron raised the garage door, the Toyota forlornly showed him its new nose job. A strip of hood, about three inches wide by one-and-a-half feet long, looked as though it had tried to slip under a truck.

Needless to say, it was time for "toughlove." In addition to paying for damages done and no driving until the car is repaired, Dave is required to pay for his own insurance. That is, if he can get the coverage.

COMBATING CAR FEVER

I know many parents who share similar frightening and frustrating stories regarding the "driven teen." Car fever is a disease. What can parents do to keep the affected kids from killing themselves or others before they start to drive wisely?

As I mentioned before, in our state, kids are issued a learner's permit at the age of fifteen and a half. They are allowed to apply for a license and complete testing at sixteen.

As a parent full of concern and love for my teenagers, I'd like to see a change in the law. How does extended training (like a full year) grab you? Perhaps the age for acquiring a driver's license should be raised to seventeen, or better still, eighteen.

On our own, we prolonged Dave's training, but peer pressure made him feel deprived. If everyone had to wait, we wouldn't be labeled HEARTLESS anymore.

Maybe you're one of the people who really appreciates the fact that your teenagers can drive themselves all over town. It saves wear and tear on your nerves and soothes your hectic life-style. True, teenagers who chauffeur themselves around offer parents a convenience.

On the other hand, parents who chauffeur with a positive attitude find themselves with anywhere from five minutes to a half-hour or more communication time. Where else but in a car can you give or receive so much concentrated time, just for talking? It's pretty hard to disappear in a car.

It's an idea. If we are *the people* who make laws, and are truly concerned about teenage drivers, maybe we should push for change.

In the meantime, there's little to do but establish and enforce your own rules and restrictions—and pray.

Car fever can be extremely contagious. At our house, Dave insists the bug is out of his system, but I'm afraid Caryl has been bitten. "What do you mean, I have to wait till I'm seventeen. The law says. . . ."

(Sigh.)

"Count it all joy. . . ."

HOW TO DEPARENT IN THE FAST LANE

1. Convince the driving instructor to fail your kid, until you feel he or she is ready for the responsibility.

2. Set restrictions and limitations that are enforced with logical consequences. When dealing with the "driving force," strong-willed parents can mean the difference between life and death.

3. Understand that a Driver's Education class teaches *how to drive,* but it does not change attitudes. A passing grade doesn't mean the student is ready for the streets. Use your own judgment. (If your child is an unsafe or potentially dangerous driver, keep the keys and pray for maturity.)

4. Lobby for new laws in licensing:
   a. To extend the driver's training period to a full year.
   b. Raise the age requirement to eighteen.
(In our state, the driver must be sixteen and have completed a Driver's Education class, or be eighteen.)

5. Try to instill in your teenager the realization that there are more important things in life than a car: like people; like relationships; like their own life.

6. Pray—and keep your insurance payments up.

14

Breaking Away

While stumbling through the major irritations of life with my teenagers, I've learned something very important: *I can cope.* I've learned how to utilize the six essential strategies: a positive attitude; the ability to find joy in all things; turning weakness into strength; and being real. Also, I've learned how to be a good loser, and found the key to unconditional love. I know now, without a doubt, I'll survive. How do I know?

Ha! Listen, such an ordeal I went through—the worst yet—and I'm still here. Not only that, I finally figured out how to cope and deparent with a lot less guilt.

Also, I came to the conclusion that if my teenagers are headstrong and determined to do things their way, or fall to strong peer pressure, they are usually unstoppable. At times such as these there isn't much a parent can do but pray.

"DEAR MOM: I'M GOING ON A TRIP"

So, I pray. I pray for their protection, for someone to reach them. Ron and I came to a "nothing to do but pray" place in early August. I call it "The California Excursion."

Dave and his best friend, Grant, started Sunday off with a trip to church. Dave's plans for the evening included spending the night at Grant's. Monday morning a phone call for Grant indicated we parents had been had. The boys were up to something.

A quick check of Dave's room revealed a note. As I read, a combination of fear, love, and anger forced me to tears.

Mom, Dad—

I am going on a trip, but don't worry. I'll be back in time to go to school. I am not running away, so don't think of it that way.

I just need to do this. I won't get into trouble, because I'll handle each problem, thinking how God or you would handle it.

Please don't worry about me, because God will be with me, and you taught me well enough to know right and wrong.

(Ulcers don't help, so trust in God to take care of me like He always has and will.)

And please don't be mad.

So just think of it as a learning experience for me that is necessary.

I love you both very much and don't worry. I'll be ok and I love you both very much.

DAVE

I wanted to cry, to scream, but I didn't. Calm won out for the moment. In numb mechanical motion, I showed the note to Ron. "At least he let us know. It's a nice letter."

"Hmmm. . . . *Something he has to do.*"

A call to his friends brought few clues to the boys' disappearance. Dave's girl friend had talked with him the night before. "I've been so worried about Dave. He said they were going to California."

Great! No food, no car, no sleeping bags. Grant had money, but how far could they go on eighty dollars?

NOT GUILTY!

Fear, anxiety, and worry ran rampant. However, in all my confusion, I noticed something was missing. *Guilt.* I didn't feel guilty. For a brief moment I rejoiced. Not *guilty!* And Satan couldn't convince me otherwise. One major battle won, but another raged inside me. The conquest faded as my thoughts returned to Dave and his friend. I cried out in anger:

God, get him! He's the one who should be suffering, not me. He's the one who should be punished.

You bet I'm angry! But, oh, Lord, keep him safe. Please keep him safe. Hold him in Your hands and build a hedge of thorns around him [Hosea 2:6].

I can't find the good in this, Lord. I'm trying. I really don't need any more illustrations for this book. It's almost finished, and I thought I've been very compassionate. Okay, Lord, if You're telling me I have to experience the pain of the hurting parent before I can identify, I get the message. I hurt ... too much. So, will You send Dave home now? Please.

Dave reassured us he'd be back. He left us a note. These were the positive threads I clung to. We tried to find him. The authorities offered no help. They informed us we could register the boys under missing persons, but they wouldn't conduct a search. The only way the boys could be picked up was if they'd committed a crime. "It is not a crime to run away in our state," the policeman said, and kindly added, "I'm sorry."

It should be a crime. Look at all the trouble those two have caused their parents. With nothing left to do, we waited and prayed.

PRAYER'S SOOTHING POWER

Pray! I almost forgot. I called every friend in town who knew how to pray. We cried and shared and prayed together. With all that help, I knew my prayers would be answered, but when? Many times, God's timetable and my patience conflict—miserably.

As I stumbled through the day, thoughts of David and Grant never left my mind. A numbness felt in the loss of a loved one crept through me and lingered. I moved. I worked. I would not allow a runaway to run me down to despair. The word *rejoice* echoed through my mind. I couldn't. Then knowing God would understand, I said, "You go ahead Lord; do it for me. I'll catch up."

Darkness brought renewed fears—intensified. Is he safe? Where will they sleep? He'll be cold—the kid forgot his jacket. What will they eat? The still, quiet darkness brought back pain, that choking agonizing pain.

I tried to think of Jesus. Sometimes, if I'm troubled I focus on Him and I can sleep. My heart wound tight, like a bomb, ready to explode. Tears formed behind tight-closed eyelids . . . too many . . . they rushed to freedom, spilling down my cheeks unto my pillow.

"The Lord is my shepherd. . . ." I repeated the psalm over and over, until the repetitions finally brought sleep.

Upon waking, I felt peace, as though nothing had happened. Then, moments later, reality struck with its knife-sharp pain. Another day of prayer. Still numb, I moved a little easier than the day before. "Trust God," I remembered my friend's words. Of course. What else could I do? I didn't even cry until I saw the old bumper sticker: HAVE YOU HUGGED YOUR KID TODAY?

"Lord," I cried, "it's not fair. I'd love to hug my kid today—if I could find him."

MIRACLE OF MIRACLES

Day Three. The pain lessened but numbness remained. Sometime in the late afternoon, the phone announced the long-awaited call. Dave—from Fort Bragg, California. The tale he spun emerged as an unbelievable miracle.

The boys had taken a bus to the coast, then hitchhiked.

"This really nice guy picked us up at Seaside and dropped us off at Newport. Then we met this other guy in a restaurant and had breakfast with him. He was on vacation, heading south. He just kind of took us along with him. We've been having devotions and praying and dumb stuff like that. He's a youth counselor—and a priest."

A priest! I could hardly believe it. "Lord," I sighed, "You really know how to take care of Your kids."

"Dave," I said, turning my attention back to my wayward son, "When are you coming home?"

"Ah ... I don't know ... maybe about three days. We're going back up the coast tomorrow. Man, this is great. Grant and me are having a blast."

"We've been worried about you."

"Mom, I told you not to worry. God always takes care of me."

"It's not that easy Dave. When you love someone, you're naturally concerned for his safety."

"Yeah. Well, I gotta go. See you Saturday or Sunday."

As I hung up the phone, I had another strong word with God.

How could You let him have fun, God? You were supposed to punish him. You know—teach him a few hard lessons. How could You let him get by with this?

Even though God and I didn't quite agree on His handling of the situation, Ron and I were both relieved. A priest. No one will believe this one. We laughed. Laughter felt good. I'd gone for three days with hardly a smile. Joy touched me with new life.

Today, with Dave finally safe at home, I'm not a hurting parent. Tomorrow—who knows? A kid can change colors and direction as easily as a chameleon.

A LOOK BACKWARD

Already, I see the good in The California Excursion. God used it to teach me to trust Him. He showed me pain and helped me understand even more clearly the need for His strength in my survival. Even my anger toward Dave for his insensitivity to our hurts subsided, as I remembered the hurts I must have caused my parents years ago. In my quest for reality, I wanted Dave to know, not only that he had hurt us, but also that we still love him and understand his unquenchable thirst for freedom. So, I told him a story:

When I was a little girl, I loved my father. Daddy was the smartest man in the world. He helped me make mud pies and spoke two languages. Daddy sailed to America from Sweden. He couldn't be home much when I was small, because he suffered from tuberculosis and lived in a sanitarium. But, when he came home, we talked and laughed and made wishes.

When I turned twelve, my dad and I built a house. I loved my dad and I loved Jesus.

Then something happened. I had passed through the seventh, eighth, and ninth grades. My father only went through the sixth grade. He didn't understand these modern times. Things were different from when he grew up. Who was he to tell me when I should date or what to do? I already knew. I was a Christian. Of course, I attended church every Sunday. He only went on Easter and Christmas. I didn't like my father very much, but I still loved Jesus.

Oh, the Bible told me to honor my father and mother, and I would, but I didn't have to love him.

Hate built a wall between Dad and me. It grew thicker and taller with every year, until ... finally, when school ended, when marriage became reality, along with a baby, I tried to tear down that wall. It wouldn't fall. Satan and I had built it too strong. I wanted to love my dad, but I couldn't. I didn't know God could.

Other relationships I had developed, with my mother, my husband, children, and God, faded. Not in a day—more like ten years. In the end, all the love I thought I had, had emptied out of me and I became a shell. I didn't love anyone, especially not myself. And, I wondered, is God real?

Then God showed me Himself. He poured His love back into me. I accepted. He filled me up, nourished me, and in His love I came back to love Him, myself, my family, and my father. Three years later Daddy died. I thank God for tearing down the wall, so I could say, "Daddy, I love you."

Now I feel the pain Mom and Dad must have felt when I turned away, ruthless and unloving, from their wise and loving counsel. As my children reach the age of turning, I feel the pull as the cycle continues.

Every child pulls away. If they didn't, parents would be stuck with kids forever, and we'd never get anywhere. I don't want you hanging around till you're forty. You need to grow and develop into a responsible adult. As you pull away, I want to leave you with a memory. No matter what happens, we love you, and God loves you.

"That was a good story, Mom," Dave offered thoughtfully.

I hugged him. And you know what? He hugged me back. I've got the entry right here in my journal.

August 15—Today David hugged me. Then you know what he did? He said, "I love you, too, Mom."

Hmmm . . . it looks like pulling away can sometimes bring you closer together.

ACCEPTING THE NORMAL

Dave's California Excursion did more than draw us together. It finally made me realize that breaking away and deparenting is a normal part of the parent-teenager relationship. The sooner I accepted the fact and turned loose, the better able I was to put the rest of my life in order. Hanging on to an independent, strong-willed teenager weakens and drains the strongest parent.

I'm too vital to go down the drain, so I backed off. These days, I feel pretty good about myself as a parent. God and I have worked out an equitable solution to my problem of letting go. I realize there are areas in which I can release my children, and I do so with joy. But, God lets me hold on when I feel the youngsters may be getting into dangerous territory. Providing I understand God is in control, I do what I can, and pray when I can't.

To deparent gradually is usually instinctive and doesn't require too much training on our part. What does take some preparation is the adjustment to our changing role. I look forward to my youngsters' departure as a positive step for Ron and me. When our parent/controller job is finished, we can move into a new life—free at last!

But, are we ever really free? I like what George Bernard Shaw says about independence in *Pygmalion:* "Independence? That's middle-class blasphemy. We are all dependent on one another, every soul of us on earth." How true. Even more, we are all ultimately dependent on God.

Independent or not, most of us parents will find ourselves facing the "empty nest"—unless you do what a dear friend of mine did. She couldn't bear the thought, so they had another baby. They parent five in all. The first is ready to leave home as the fifth arrives. Don't laugh; it *is* an alternative. Me? I prefer the deparenting process now.

To me, there is nothing sadder than to see a family fall apart in divorce, once the children are gone and Mom and Dad discover, "Everything we had for each other is gone. The kids have grown. They don't need us anymore. There is nothing left but an empty house."

METHODS FOR STAYING IN LOVE

In the chapter titled "Love Your Teenager as Yourself," we discussed the importance of a love relationship between husband and wife. This is where we put the concept into play.

For the eighteen years of our marriage, Ron and I have tried to value our husband-wife relationship, even above the relationship we share with our children.

Think of it. Soon our children will leave and build families of their own. Although our family ties will remain strong, the relationship left to hold "home" together will be ours—husband and wife. Therefore, my priority is to maintain and fulfill our present and future together.

If, by chance, you're wondering how, I'll be glad to share a few of our methods for staying in love. We still date each other; we take vacations, at least once a year—away from the kids. Sound romantic? In addition, we spend time together nearly everyday, usually in the form of walks and talks; then we reminisce, dream of our future, and discuss strategies for handling our children. Our love for each other fills the emptiness caused by the evacuating teenager.

WHAT ABOUT THE SINGLE PARENT?

While the husband and wife combine to make an excellent team in combating the forces of teenagism as they fill the emptying nest with their love, there is an exception: the plight of the single parent.

There are many instances when parents, whether by divorce or death, find themselves in the single-parent role. A case in point is the tragedy which occurred in a family we know. The family seemed as ideal as some of those "perfect" television clans. Apparently, it wasn't enough for Bob, the husband-father member of the Sanders' family. A successful businessman, Bob became dissatisfied with what he called "the dull, dreary existence of family-style living." With *himself* in mind, he decided to extend his family to include a younger woman. His faithful and devoted wife of twenty-five years tried counseling, understanding, and forgiveness for over a year. After losing thirty pounds, her good health, and a large portion of self-esteem, Susan acknowledged defeat and divorce as the only alternative. Her prize? Two teenagers to rear alone. Much against her will, Susan joined the ranks of the single parent.

Therefore, if the husband-wife team clashes and disintegrates in the midst of the parent-teen conflict and deparenting time, who does the single parent call on for assistance?

God offers special help to the lonely, the widow, and the fatherless. ". . . the hapless commits himself to thee; thou hast been the helper of the fatherless" (Psalms 10:14). God will provide comfort.

Another source of comfort for the single parent (and married parents as well) is the accumulation of friends. Although I briefly covered these friendships in chapter 8, I'd again like to stress their importance.

Develop friendships with people who share similar interests—those who have teenagers of their own—with whom you can comfortably "share one another's burdens." In the burden bearing, lasting friendships may unfold. These relationships, I believe, are essential in the successful future life of a deparenter.

DEPARENT WITHOUT DEVASTATION

1. Keep telling yourself, "I can cope with anything," and "I *will* survive." These positive statements will give you reassurance. Don't forget to ask for God's help. Although there are many areas we fail when we try to do it all ourselves, with God we can make it.

2. If married, move closer to your spouse. A romantic candlelight dinner for two. Plan quiet, nonstressful times together— often.

3. If single, develop close friendships, where burden sharing is an equitable part of the relationship.

4. Build yourself up by developing outside interests. This is not a time in your life to be falling apart, but, rather, a time to pull yourself together.

For a good reading and self-help book consider: *Ruby Mac-Donald's Forty-Plus and Feeling Fabulous Book.*

5. Keep reminding your children you love them. They may need the reassurance when your attention wanes. Explain that you are planning for (looking forward to) their departure, because you realize they must mature and lead their own lives as adult members of society.

6. Base your relationships with yourself, your family, and friends on God's unconditional love and grace. Be assured of a happy ending—eventually.

Epilogue:

Feathering the Empty Nest

So now you are looking forward to a new era in your life! It will take some planning for the transition. Areas of help may be found in hobbies, returning to school, and careers. While our children are consumed with breaking away, we can assume an exciting, new identity as a retired parent. I've chosen pottery and writing as my chief interests, and, as you know, work part-time as a nurse. Oh, I'm still around when the kids need me; I'm just trying to give them a little more room to grow.

With all these activities and interests occupying my mind, I figure Satan won't be able to rob me of my vitality by blowing up my guilt, worry, anxiety, and fear. And would you believe it? When I dove into projects and plans minus the children, they relaxed their eager efforts for freedom. Since I started running my affairs instead of theirs, I see more of them than ever.

While I've had my share of parenting problems, I wouldn't trade places with any other mother in the world—mostly because things wouldn't be much different. God would have had to teach me the same lessons regardless. And look how much I've gained. I rarely feel guilty anymore. I packed up all those home-brewed guilts and popped the lid down tight. They get to rumbling every once in a while, but I just sit on them to keep them under control. These days I hardly ever think negative for more than a couple of hours at a time—it's great how we can lift ourselves out of the pits, just by changing our thought processes. Joy comes easier and easier (not that I sit and laugh when things go sour!). Well . . . I do that occasionally, too, but mostly, it's knowing God's hand is right there making me better. My teenagers have caused me to develop inner strength. Because of them, I had to admit failure as the mythical model parent. And, what better mode could God have used to teach me the value in suffering than with my own children? Nothing else means as much. Then there's *love*. If not for my teenagers, the challenge to seek pure unconditional love might never have presented itself.

It was that love and the love God gives His children, even when we hurt Him, that prompted me to share the story about my dad and me with my runaway son. I wanted to instill a lasting memory of my love and God's love in both David and Caryl. So, along with the story I told David, I wrote and sang this song just for Caryl and him.

REMEMBER HOW I LOVE YOU

When you were still a child,
   you needed us a while,
But time came as you grew older, you grew bolder.
You stepped out on your own,
   pushed the love that you had known
Behind the empty dream of freedom's song.

Now you look at me with eyes
   that say, "I'm older and so wise,
And I don't need you to tell me what to do."
Eyes that sometimes flash with hate,
   I pray my words are not too late—
Can they penetrate the heart that's turned away?

I'm reminded of a child of God,
    who wandered far from home;
Far from loving arms that held her safe, secure.
Independence was the name
    of the foolish, childish game
I played outside the echo of God's song.

Then one day His words rang clear;
    soft as music to my ear,
And I turned from freedom's fantasy to sing them.
As I came to sing my part,
    His love poured in my heart
And I'll sing His song of love forevermore.

Chorus:
Just remember how I love you,
    my daughter and my son,
And how a mother's love is never, never done.
O remember how He loves you,
    my daughter and my son,
For your Father's love is never, never done.

Words and Music by Patricia Rushford
© 1981

"Mom, I know you love me," Dave spoke thoughtfully. "But, you know, I've been thinking. Now ... I'm not being disrespectful or anything like that. It's just ... well ... after serious consideration, I've come to a conclusion about parents."

"Hmmm ... and what's that Dave," I said thinking, *at last, we're going to have a real conversation.*

"When grown-ups, especially parents, get to be about thirty-five or so, they start getting a little looney."

I almost raised my voice in objection, caught myself and laughed instead. *Maybe he's right,* I thought, *it takes a small degree of insanity to rear teenagers and come up smiling.*

Suggested Reading List

Brody, Jane, *Jane Brody's Nutrition Book* (New York: W. W. Norton & Co., Inc., 1981)

Dobson, James, *Hide or Seek* (Old Tappan, N.J.: Fleming H. Revell Company, 1979 Revised)

———— *The Strong-Willed Child* (Wheaton, Ill.: Tyndale House Publishers, 1978)

———— *Emotions: Can You Trust Them?* (Ventura, Calif.: Regal Books, 1980). See Part I.

Lewis, C. S., *The Problem of Pain* (New York: Macmillan Publishing Co., Inc., 1948)

Narramore, Bruce and Counts, Bill, *Freedom from Guilt* (Irvine, Calif.: Harvest House Publishers, 1974)

Narramore, Bruce, *Adolescence Is Not an Illness* (Old Tappan, N.J.: Fleming H. Revell Company, 1980)

MacDonald, Ruby, *Ruby MacDonald's Forty-Plus and Feeling Fabulous Book* (Old Tappan, N.J.: Fleming H. Revell Company, 1982)

Swindoll, Charles R., *You and Your Child* (Nashville: Thomas Nelson Inc. Publishers, 1977)

Tournier, Paul, *Guilt and Grace* (New York: Harper & Row, 1962)